Avallon

Époisses

Chagny

Dijon

Vougeot

Tournus

Rully

Chablis

Solutré

Arnay
~le~Duc

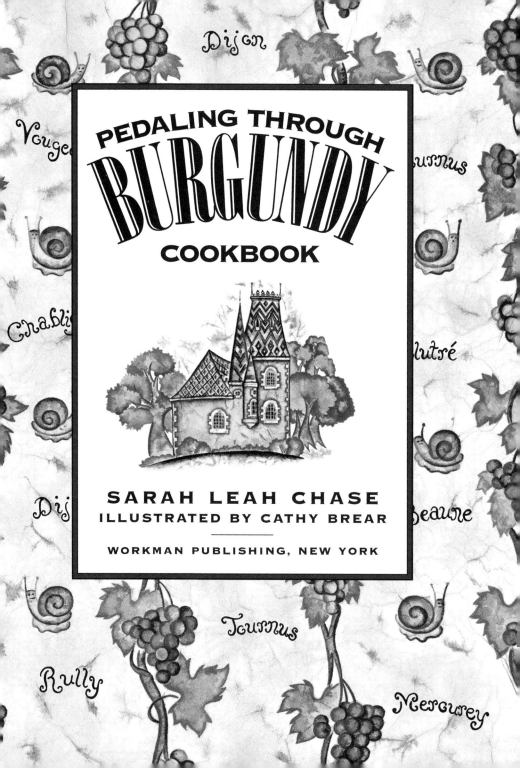

PEDALING THROUGH
BURGUNDY
COOKBOOK

SARAH LEAH CHASE
ILLUSTRATED BY CATHY BREAR

WORKMAN PUBLISHING, NEW YORK

Thanks to the following for permission to use the excerpts selected for this book: Page 92: Excerpted with the permission of Prentice-Hall Press, a Division of Simon & Schuster Inc., from *Long Ago in France* by M.F.K. Fisher. Copyright © 1991 by Prentice Hall Press. Page 157: *The Heartbreak Grape: A California Winemaker's Search for the Perfect Pinot Noir* by Marq de Villiers. Copyright © 1994 by Jacobus Communication Corp. Reprinted by permission of HarperCollins Publisher, New York. Page 175: *Puligny-Montrachet: Journal of a Village in Burgundy* by Simon Loftus. Copyright © 1993 by Simon Loftus. Reprinted by permission of Alfred A. Knopf, Inc., New York.

Library of Congress Cataloging-in-Publication Data
Chase, Sarah Leah.
Pedaling Through Burgundy cookbook / by Sarah Leah Chase;
illustrations by Cathy Brear.
p.   cm.
Includes index.
ISBN 1-56305-359-4
1. Cookery, French.   2. Cookery—France—Burgundy.
3. Bicycle touring—France—Burgundy.   4. Burgundy (France)—Description and travel.   I. Title.
TX719.C4244 1995   95-32829
641.59444—dc20   CIP

Cover design by Lisa Hollander
Book design by Lisa Hollander with Lori S. Malkin
Cover and book illustrations by Cathy Brear

Workman books are available at special discounts when purchased in bulk for premium and sales promotions as well as for fund-raising or educational use. Special editions or book excerpts can also be created to specification. For details, contact the Special Sales Director at the address below.

Workman Publishing Company, Inc.
708 Broadway
New York, NY 10003-9555

First printing October 1995
10 9 8 7 6 5 4 3 2 1

FOR RICHARD MEECH, who was the first to design a bicycling tour in Burgundy and who introduced me to Sartre, Camus, and Clos de Tart all in the same year. May existentialism and hedonism continue to commingle forever after.

Acknowledgments

I prefer to write autobiographical cookbooks, in which the recipes spring from personal experience as opposed to being created purely for the purpose of writing a cookbook. Having authored and co-authored four cookbooks over the last ten years, I found myself feeling spent and as if I had related my life's entire stoveside story up to the date of its thirtysomething point. I was intending to get on with the non-culinary business of living. But then Peter Workman suggested the irresistible idea of my writing a series of smaller cookbooks inspired by my yearly bicycling forays through delectable regions of Europe. I had taken these trips working as a cycling guide for the Canada-based touring company Butterfield & Robinson. The company's founder and president, George Butterfield, an avid food and wine connoisseur, greeted this idea with immediate enthusiasm and lent the sort of behind-the-scenes support any quirkily creative person would pray to receive. Words alone cannot express the magnitude of gratitude I feel toward both Peter and George for being the vital, yet mostly silent, backbone of this culinary venture.

Working on this *Pedaling Through Burgundy Cookbook* has provided me with the renewed opportunity to strengthen bonds of admiration and friendship at both Workman Publishing and Butterfield &

Robinson. I remain, as always, indebted to my editor, Suzanne Rafer, for her uniquely diplomatic dishing out of criticism and praise alike. At the same time, I'm especially grateful to my agent Doe Coover for always lending a calming voice to my book-induced roller-coaster angst and elation. I've really enjoyed getting closer to Lisa Hollander and Lori Malkin in Workman's art department and being allowed to offer snippets of input to the vibrant illustrations Cathy Brear created for this book. I can scarcely contain my delight over its beautiful design.

vi

Nicola Speakman, in Butterfield & Robinson's Toronto office, has truly worked miracles of travel scheduling for me, and I am most thankful. The team at Butterfield & Robinson's Beaune headquarters has been immensely helpful and informative and to Victoria Bake and Nathalie Bichot I extend one huge *merci beaucoup*. Another grand *merci* is due Chantal Leroux for so joyfully helping me see and taste Burgundy's rich cuisine through the eyes and palate of a native. Thanks, too, to Athlyn Fitz-James, Tom Hamilton, and Terry Price for all their special insights into life in Beaune.

I would also like to take this opportunity to thank the men who have each in their own way been the most memorable of co-guides and traveling companions throughout my varied bicycling adventures in Burgundy. *Je t'embrasse* Richard Meech, David Young, and Nigel Dyche. Extra, extra *baisers* are due to Nigel, my fiancé, who valiantly sacrificed waistline vanities for at least a month of Sundays in the service of helping me perfect the recipe for *oeufs en meurette*. Now, there's all the more of you to marry!

Contents

Burgundy Beginnings

....

MODERATION IN MODERATION.
—A French saying which I adore

....

To lovers of food and wine, the mention of Burgundy almost always brings to mind the sublime taste of the region's world-famous wines. The vineyards that produce the grapes for these wines spring, somewhat astonishingly, from myriad soils and microclimates in a breathtakingly beautiful thirty-mile stretch known as the Côte d'Or, or "Slope of Gold." Of course, Burgundy, once France's grandest and richest duchy, also offers a tremendous kaleidoscope of visual and intellectual feasts. Yet, there is something in the mystery and mystique of the vines that cling to the Côte d'Or that makes them the perfect symbol of the province and of my personal relationship to it.

Burgundian-born Colette wrote, "the vine gives us true understanding of the savor of the earth," and so divinely regarded is that earthy savor in Burgundy, it is literally against the law to water one's grapevines in the face of drought. Mother Nature and chance charmingly rule the old-fashioned world of Burgundy viticulture. Indeed, Burgundians believe a vine should struggle a little now and again to yield the sort of flavor-intense grape that produces the finest wine. And, curiously enough, it was a similarly metaphorical combination of chance and struggle that first led me to bicycle in Burgundy's Côte d'Or.

The trail of my Burgundy initiation can be traced back to my senior year at an all-girl high school, where my one-track mind focused not on the lack of the opposite sex, but on bicycling through Europe. Up until that point in my life, I had been a scrupulous saver, but now I became determined to take my eighteen years of life savings—from every allowance, odd job, and birthday windfall—and consign it all to funding a dream summer abroad with a knapsack and ten-speed bicycle. I can still vividly remember inserting coins into a pay phone in response to an advertisement I had seen for a six-week student bicycle trip between Vienna and Paris organized by Butterfield & Robinson, a Toronto-based travel company. Even more vividly, I remember struggling to convince my bachelor uncle, as he sipped his third glass of my mother's cooking sherry, what a good investment in the future it would be to part with the additional three hundred dollars I needed for this venture. Chance, like the perfect amount of sunshine and rainfall in a rare vintage year for Burgundy wine, conspired to put my uncle in a magnanimous mood and thereby me, excitedly, on my first transatlantic flight.

Naturally, once abroad, I visited all the most famous sites, but it was the less grandiose experiences gained from pedaling through the tradition-rich countryside that truly sealed my love for specialized European travel. In a short six weeks, I became a convert to exploring Europe at the slow yet exquisitely exhilarating and private pace afforded by a bicycle. That summer of cycling became more than a youthful passing passion; it emerged as a pivotal point in the path my life would take. For once I returned home to begin college, persistence and enthusiasm would soon win me a coveted summer job of guide for the very same Butterfield & Robinson student bicycle tours. And I continued on as a guide for three more adventuresome, challenging, and remarkable European summers.

Graduation from college, and the reality of making a living in the "real world," spelled the all-to-soon end to such fantasy months abroad. Beyond cycling, I knew I loved to cook, and so began to ponder if the exciting foods discovered during my European jaunts could now fuel more than that long day's worth of vigorous cycling. It struck me that there just might be a way of turning experiences of palatable pedaling into some form of profitable peddling. The combination of biking and eating in France always fired my culinary imagination with the greatest satisfaction. I especially liked the shops called *traiteurs,* where all sorts of delicious ready-made soups, salads, and main-dish entrées abounded. I reasoned that if I could bring this aspect of the food of my travels to a specialty shop on my beloved island of Nantucket, I might just manage to live happily ever after stateside. My *traiteur*-style shop, Que Sera Sarah was thus born, and filled with all the personally imprinted, eclectic discoveries of my bicycling days.

Catering life for awhile seemed as rosy as a slice of country pâté until one day, a few seasons along, a convergence of refrigerators breaking down and young summer employees suddenly departing brought on overwhelming stress. Not surprisingly, I longed for that feeling of youthful freedom that had once come from meandering by bicycle past centuries-old churches or coasting between orderly vineyard landscapes. Again I phoned Butterfield & Robinson to inquire if they were in need of any slightly rusty guiding services for their newly developed adult European biking tours.

Good fortune was to come my way on this otherwise angst-ridden August day of 1984, as within hours of my phone call, Butterfield & Robinson had me scheduled to lead a ten-day, mid-September bicycle trip through Burgundy. Elated, I impulsively closed my shop, posting the following sign on the door: "In a rare deviation from my favorite color of pink, Que Sera Sarah has fled to Burgundy! See you in two weeks."

Eleven years have passed since I guided that first adult trip in Burgundy and during this time I have also led French and Italian bicycle tours in many regions. There honestly is not one area I prefer over another, though Burgundy remains dearest to my heart because it was my 1984 trip there that established what would soon evolve into the most fulfilling of complementary off-season, side careers. The decision therefore to feature Burgundy as a kick-off to a threesome of small cookbooks devoted to recipes inspired by my bicycle guiding tours abroad, emerged as a sentimentally logical one (if such an oxymoronic concept can exist!).

For the cyclist, Burgundy presents itself as a distillation of the dreamiest aspects of French rural tradition. The landscape is one of vast vineyards, sinuous rivers and streams, and peaceful cow and goat pastures dotted with snug little stone hamlets, elegant châteaux, and the occasional imposing medieval castle crowned with glistening harvest-hued Flemish tiles. Many of the land's traditions and sites appear doubly novel to North American travelers on the tours I lead because bicycling casts a magical spell when combined with exploring unknown and foreign pockets of intrigue. Such seems to reawaken a childlike innocence in even the toughest of successful movers and shakers.

As might well be expected, the food in Burgundy remains some of the richest and most heartily traditional in all of France. Lunches can easily last for three hours and dinners for five, and ingredients like double cream, unpasteurized cheeses, butter, bacon, and beef are revered rather than reviled. Wine is omnipresent, beer frosty and thirst quenching, and coffee caffeinated. Biking here does indeed have a way of instilling a keen appetite on many levels for all things Burgundian. So, of course, the total cycling experience inevitably involves guiltless indulgence in regional specialties, of which the mere mention at home would be cause enough for cardiac arrest.

As a cookbook author and guide, I have always felt it my duty to taste and become familiar with as many regional dishes as possible. Since the week-long tours I have led in Burgundy are by design concentrated in the small area of the Côte d'Or, I have made a point of exploring additional departments on my own in order to present a broader overview of the entire region's cuisine. The cumulative years I have spent cooking, dining, and reading and writing about food have conspired to turn me into an opinionated cook and have given me the confidence to adapt recipes to my own preferences. Recipes remain totally true to their origins only if I think the final result is worth the calories or the time-consuming labor.

Frequently, however, I have taken a Burgundian notion and infused it with my own sensibilities. For example, I'm crazy for the Burgundy bottled crème de cassis from Domaine Jacob (a favorite cycling stop) but once I have a souvenir stash back in my Nantucket kitchen, I can't resist drizzling the inky elixir into a few not strictly Burgundian creations. But since it is Burgundy cassis that lends the exceptional flavor to the recipe, I feel justified in including it in this collection of recipes. In this way, I have written this book as more of a poetically licensed, culinary homage to my bicycle travels in Burgundy and not a disciplined documentation of totally authentic Burgundian cooking.

Bicycling in Burgundy is many things, but above all it is fun, and I in turn have strived to capture that spirit by making this cookbook fun. People love to pick up and spike their conversations with key or melodic sounding foreign phrases when they travel. I have intentionally used a combination of French and English in naming the dishes in this book

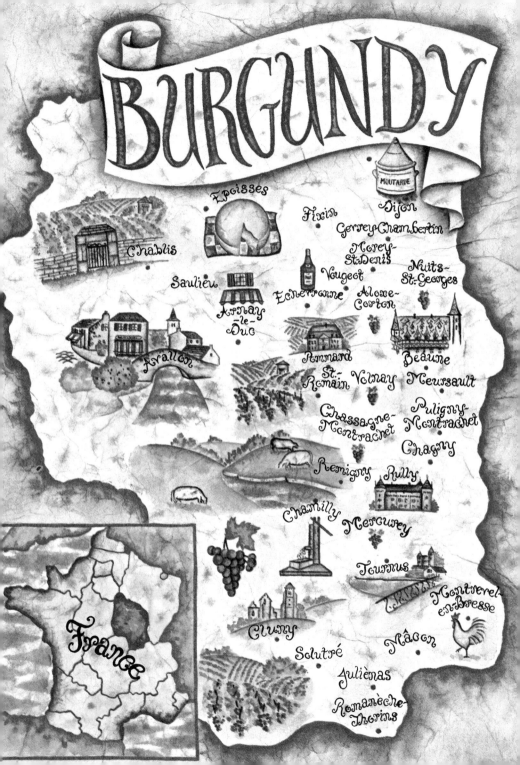

....

WHENEVER I THINK of the joy of living, the pleasure of a perfect dish served with a perfect wine and the deep joy that comes from perfect harmony, I see Burgundy. . . . The song of the world grabs me—I know I am in the right place to enjoy life.

—MIREILLE JOHNSTON, THE CUISINE OF THE ROSE

....

to reflect symbolically what I love to see happen when English and French sensibilities come together to create the most delectable of worlds and recipes.

I am a person who travels with my eyes, ears, and mouth open, and my primary insight into a place often begins with getting a grasp on its food. I'm much better at remembering the tastes of my travels than at taking reams and rolls of photographs for future reminiscing. There's nothing I enjoy more than enlightening friends on my myriad expeditions by inviting them over to share in a dinner that celebrates my latest flavor and ingredient enthusiasms. It is my hope this book will make it irresistible for those lucky enough to have been fellow cyclists or travelers in Burgundy to do the same. May it also take those who prefer armchair cooking, cycling, or traveling on one mouth-watering culinary journey, as well as inspire a bountiful bevy of wine-tasting dinners.

When I reflect on Burgundian food, I remind myself of an insightful dining experience with my Beaunois neighbor Chantal, at a charming, rustic farmhouse restaurant. I had begun the meal with a fabulous green salad accompanied by slabs of toasted French bread oozing pungent melted Epoisses cheese. Next came juicy, mustard-coated pork chops grilled over the hearth. Traditionally a cheese course would follow, but when I protested, citing all the cheese I had already consumed with my salad, Chantal dismissed my concerns by advising that the course should still be ordered *"pour la plaisir,"* or solely for the pleasure of it. No wonder bicycling in Burgundy has made me an eager convert to the French axiom "Moderation in moderation." I, of course, now know that Mireille Johnston knew whereof she spoke when wisely declaring Burgundy is the "right place to enjoy life."

AMUSE-BOUCHES
AND THEN SOME

Tarte aux Escargots de Chantal

MOUTARDE

Oysters with Chablis Cream

Shallot & Walnut Croûtes

RULLY · VOUGEOT · GILLY-LES-CITEAUX · MERCUREY · CLUNY · FIXIN

Every weeklong cycling adventure that I lead in Burgundy begins with an afternoon warm-up ride through the surrounding, fertile countryside. Sometimes, we first become acquainted with our gears, brakes, and spokes in a blissful pedal through the world-famous vineyards of Puligny- and Chassagne-Montrachet. Other times, we breeze through pastoral farmlands, with a local goat cheese tasting as our pungent destination.

When it comes to beloved mealtimes, *amuse-bouches* appear as the irresistible, edible equivalent to the scenic tease of these warm-up rides. The term translates literally and charmingly as an amusement or entertainment for the mouth, in preparation for more fantastic fare to come. In restaurants, the *amuse-bouche* will often be an exquisite and savory morsel—a complimentary offering from the chef to the diners as they contemplate the menu. In this chapter, the concept is broadened to include both petite and grander appetite titillations.

Gougères

Gougères, savory, fluffy, golden pastries laced with small cubes of nutty Gruyère cheese, are the quintessential Burgundian hors d'oeuvre. These warm little mouthfuls were originally served at wine tastings to complement yet not compete with the taste of Burgundy wines. Now they almost always appear with an apéritif, kir or otherwise, at hotels and restaurants throughout the region. And no local festivity seems complete without an aromatic basket of freshly baked *gougères* on the scene.

In Burgundy, they would never think of making anything but the traditional Gruyère-flavored *gougère,* but once the vast Atlantic has separated me from the disapproving eye of rigid French traditionalists, I find all sorts of flavor creativity hard to resist.

With all due respect, here is an excellent traditional *gougère* recipe, followed rebelliously and irresistibly (I think) by some of my more successful variations.

3

> 1½ *cups water*
> 8 *tablespoons (1 stick) unsalted butter, cut into small pieces*
> 1½ *cups unbleached all-purpose flour*
> 5 *large eggs*
> 1 *heaping tablespoon imported Dijon mustard*
> *Salt and freshly ground white pepper to taste*
> *Pinch of freshly grated nutmeg*
> *Pinch of cayenne pepper*
> 1½ *cups finely diced French or Swiss Gruyère cheese*
> *Flavor options, if using (see below)*
> 3 *tablespoons milk*
> ¼ *cup finely grated Parmesan cheese*

1. Preheat the oven to 375°F. Line two 15 x 12-inch baking sheets with parchment paper.

2. Combine the water and butter in a medium-size saucepan and bring to a boil. When the butter is completely melted, remove from the heat and gradually stir in the flour until smooth. Return the pan to medium-low heat and cook, stirring constantly, until the batter is quite thick and is pulling away from the sides of the pan, 3 to 4 minutes.

3. Remove the pan from the heat again and beat in the eggs (you can use an electric hand mixer), one at a time, mixing well after each addition. Mix in the mustard and season with the salt, white pepper, nutmeg, and cayenne pepper. Finally, fold in the Gruyère and any of the flavor options, if you are using them.

4. Drop the batter by rounded heaping teaspoons onto the prepared baking sheets. Brush the top of each with a little milk and dust lightly with the Parmesan.

5. Bake the *gougères* until puffed and golden brown, 15 to 20 minutes. Serve warm, on a pretty tray or in a napkin-lined basket. (The *gougères* may also be baked ahead in a 350°F oven and reheated just before serving.)

MAKES ABOUT 50 GOUGERES

Flavor Options
Any of the following additions will flavor a batch of *gougères*:

More Mustard: Add an additional tablespoon regular Dijon mustard and 3 tablespoons coarse-grained for an extra mustardy *gougère*.

Smoked Salmon: Add 5 ounces finely diced smoked salmon and 2 tablespoons snipped fresh chives or dill.

Bacon or Ham: Add ¾ cup finely crumbled crisp bacon or minced prosciutto.

Herbs: Add ½ cup assorted minced herbs—parsley, chives, chervil, dill, and/or tarragon.

Provençal: Add 2 cloves garlic, minced, 12 minced sun-dried tomato halves, and ½ cup shredded fresh basil.

Roquefort: Substitute 1½ cups crumbled Roquefort cheese for the Gruyère in step 3.

Candied Shallot and Walnut Croûtes

I magination seems to know no bounds when it comes to conjuring up new toppings for Italian crostini and bruschetta, and I see no reason why a little creative license shouldn't be applied to the French cousin, the *croûte*. This particular topping was inspired by the flawless large shallots that I never cease to marvel at, for sale at the bustling open-air market in Beaune every Saturday morning.

The *croûtes*—toasted rounds from a French *baguette*—are topped with shallots that have been minced, sautéed, and sweetened with a drizzle of thick, purple cassis. The syrupiness of the cassis is balanced by the crunch of toasted walnuts and pungency of bits of blue cheese. Sip on a properly made kir for a fine Burgundian beginning to an evening (see page 10).

5

CROÛTES
20 rounds French bread (½ inch thick)
Olive oil for brushing

CANDIED SHALLOT TOPPING
3 tablespoons walnut oil
10 large, firm shallots, minced
2½ tablespoons crème de cassis
½ cup lightly toasted walnuts (page 72),
 chopped into ¼-inch dice
Salt and freshly ground black pepper
 to taste
4 ounces Roquefort or Saga Blue cheese (rind
 removed), crumbled

1. Preheat the oven to 400°F.

2. To make the *croûtes*, lay out the bread rounds on a baking sheet and brush the tops lightly with olive oil. Toast the *croûtes* until lightly browned and crunchy, 10 to 12 minutes. Cool and store in an airtight bag or container until ready to use, for up to 4 days.

3. To make the candied shallot topping, heat the walnut oil in a medium-size skillet over medium-high heat. Add the shallots and sauté for 5 minutes. Reduce heat to medium-low and continue to cook, stirring occasionally, until the shallots are very soft and translucent, 12 to 15 minutes more. Stir in the cassis, increase the heat to medium-high again, and cook until the shallots are slightly caramelized, 2 to 3 minutes. Remove the mixture from the heat, stir in the walnuts, and season to taste with salt and pepper. At this point, the shallot mixture may be kept at room temperature for a couple hours or stored in the refrigerator for 3 to 4 days.

4. When ready to assemble, preheat the oven to 375°F.

5. Mound a generous tablespoon of the shallot mixture over the top of each *croûte* and arrange on a baking sheet. Dot the top of each *croûte* with a few morsels of the blue cheese. Bake the *croûtes* until the cheese is melted and the *croûtes* are warmed through, 5 to 7 minutes. Arrange them on a serving platter and serve while still warm.

MAKES 20 CROUTES

Tarte Flambée d'Avallon

A March research trip to Burgundy for the purposes of this book provided a refreshingly different view than the summer and fall ones I had taken over the years. How unlike their autumn harvest glory the vineyards look in early spring when, as the winemakers say, the vines awaken and begin to "weep" their sap. There often lingers a pristine, light dusting of snow, making one hunger for warming food and cozy dining spots.

As I wended my way from Paris through the plains along the Yonne River toward the Côte d'Or, the hitherto unexplored town of Avallon beckoned as a lunch destination. As is my nature, I immediately set out to case the cobbled alleys of the town, which is lined with medieval houses and punctuated by clock towers and Romanesque churches. I was nearly resigned to contenting myself with a visual feast, as restaurants were few and I was rapidly becoming chilled to the bone, when I happened upon just the spot I had been dreaming of—Le Saint Laurent on 1 rue

7

du Marché—a little corner restaurant specializing in *tartes* cooked to order in a wood-burning oven. A *demi-carafe* of Beaujolais and a *tarte flambée*—a crisp, thin-crusted pizza with *fromage blanc,* sautéed onions, and slivers of ham—proved to be the perfect antidote to March's lionlike rawness.

Since *fromage blanc* can be hard to find in North America, my recipe approximates this fresh and fluffy French cheese by using a combination of goat cheese, ricotta, and crème fraîche. *Tarte Flambée* may be cut into either small pieces to serve as an appetizer or larger squares to make a circulation-restoring lunch or light supper.

CRUST
1 package (¼ ounce) active dry yeast
1⅓ cups warm water
1½ teaspoons sea or coarse salt
1½ tablespoons olive oil
½ cup whole wheat or rye flour
3 to 4 cups bread flour

TOPPING
3 tablespoons unsalted butter
2 large white onions, thinly sliced into rings
4 ounces creamy white goat cheese
⅔ cup ricotta cheese
½ cup crème fraîche
2 large eggs
Sea or coarse salt and freshly ground white pepper
    to taste
¼ teaspoon freshly grated nutmeg
2 ounces thinly sliced prosciutto

1. To make the crust dough, stir the yeast and water together in a large mixing bowl and proof until foamy, 5 minutes. Stir in the salt, oil, and whole wheat or rye flour. Using a wooden spoon, gradually stir in 3 cups of the bread flour. Add enough additional flour to make a moderately stiff dough. Turn out the dough onto a lightly floured surface and knead it until smooth and satiny, 5 to 7 minutes. Place the dough in a clean bowl, cover with plastic wrap or a linen kitchen towel, and let rise in a warm place until doubled in bulk, about 1½ hours.

2. Meanwhile, prepare the topping: Melt the butter over medium heat in a large skillet. Add the onions and sauté slowly until very soft and just beginning to color, about 20 minutes. Remove from the heat and set aside.

3. In a medium-size bowl, mash or beat together the goat cheese, ricotta, and crème fraîche until smooth and creamy. Beat in the eggs until thoroughly combined. Season the mixture with the salt, white pepper, and nutmeg. Set aside.

4. When ready to assemble and bake the *tarte,* preheat the oven to 375°F. Lightly oil a 15 x 10-inch baking sheet.

5. Punch down the dough and turn it out onto a lightly floured surface. Roll out into a rectangle slightly larger than the baking sheet. Transfer carefully to the pan, letting the edges of the dough hang over the edges of the pan. Spread the cheese and egg mixture evenly over the surface of the dough. Then scatter the sautéed onions evenly over the cheese. Tear the prosciutto into irregular shreds and scatter over the top of the *tarte.* Crimp the overhanging edges of dough decoratively and bake the tarte in the center of the oven until the crust is golden brown and the prosciutto pieces have become crisp, 40 to 45 minutes. Cut the hot *tarte* into pieces and serve at once.

MAKES 6 TO 8 SERVINGS AS LUNCH, MORE AS AN HORS D'OEUVRE

KIR CORRECTNESS

*I*n circles I have been known to inhabit, the cocktail order of a Kir—white wine blended with the black currant liqueur, crème de cassis—is thought best reserved for flirtatious females who frequent trendy bars. But in Burgundy, a kir is the apéritif of choice, and it is only there that I have experienced the drink as it was meant to be truly enjoyed. The mayor of Dijon from 1946 to 1968, Canon Kir, gave the cocktail its name and served it at all official receptions. *Vin blanc cassis,* however, had long been a traditional Burgundian apéritif, and M.F.K. Fisher wrote that back in Dijon in 1929 it was "a routine student's drink because it cost one franc."

Most North American bartenders add cassis to white wine as if they were adding vermouth to a very dry martini. A real kir is made by blending one part cassis to four or five parts chilled white wine, preferably Aligoté from Burgundy. The finest Aligoté is thought to be produced by Aubert de Villaine in Bouzeron. Yet, just to confuse matters, Villaine thinks his Aligoté too good to adulterate with cassis. A more robust kir can be made by mixing the same proportion of cassis with red wine, or even better, Beaujolais, for *un kir communard* or *kir rouge.*

For more advanced kir aficionados, there are different flavors of syrupy fruit liqueurs that can be similarly mixed into still or sparkling wine. My favorite *maison de cassis* is Domaine Lucien Jacob, to which we bike uphill in Echevronne to the west of Côte de Nuits vineyards. Here, Christine, a delightful Englishwoman married to Jacob's son, conducts enthusiastic tastings of the property's Crème de Cassis, Crème de Framboise (raspberry), and Crème de Mûre (blackberry). My favorite is Jacob's *mûre,* and sample bottles of all the flavors are sold in convenient gift packs. They are a popular culinary souvenir among cyclists in my groups.

Baked Oysters with Chablis Cream

∾

Since the province of Burgundy is landlocked, it obviously can't be known for its oysters. Yet oysters are so beloved by the French in general and make so perfect a match with white Burgundy wine—Chablis in particular—that they appear frequently on menus of starred restaurants throughout the region. There's even an oyster bar that has recently opened in Beaune down the street from the venerable Hotel le Cep, where my cycling groups have resided since day one.

Here's a warm recipe for those times when enough discipline can be mustered to resist slurping down copious amounts of iced oysters on the half-shell. The same Chablis that subtly flavors the cream sauce should be poured freely as an accompaniment to this refined first course.

24 just-opened oysters on the half-shell
1 tablespoon unsalted butter
2 shallots, minced
1 cup Chablis or Petit Chablis wine from Burgundy
1 cup heavy (or whipping) cream
Very tiny pinch of curry powder
Sea salt to taste
Freshly ground black pepper to taste
Several sprigs fresh watercress for garnish

1. Drain off and reserve any juices from the opened oysters. Melt the butter in a medium-size saucepan over medium heat. Add

the shallots and sauté to soften, 1 to 2 minutes. Add the Chablis and bring to a boil over medium-high heat. Cook until the wine is reduced by half, 6 to 8 minutes. Add the reserved juices from the oysters and cook for a few minutes more.

2. Strain the mixture through a sieve into a clean saucepan. Discard the solids. Add the cream, bring to a boil, and then cook again until the liquid is reduced by half, 10 to 12 minutes. While the mixture is reducing, season with the curry powder and salt. Keep the sauce warm over very low heat.

3. When ready to cook the oysters, preheat the oven to 450°F.

4. Arrange the oysters snugly, side by side, in a roasting pan. Season each with a sprinkling of freshly ground pepper. Nap each oyster with a generous tablespoon of the warm Chablis cream and bake the oysters until they are just cooked through and the cream has begun to brown slightly, 3 to 4 minutes.

5. Using tongs, arrange 4 to 6 oysters per person on individual serving plates. Place sprigs of watercress between the shells and serve immediately.

MAKES 4 TO 6 SERVINGS

C hablis with oysters is a stimulating combination that goes back at least to the tenth century, if the dating of this poetic fragment is correct:

CHABLIS IS SO GOOD WITH OYSTERS
THAT I'M TEMPTED TO LEAVE THESE CLOISTERS
AND FIND TRUE LOVE WHE'ERE I'M APT TO.
—KERMIT LYNCH
ADVENTURES ON THE WINE ROUTE

Prosciutto-Wrapped Escargots

I have never repeated a recipe from one of my other cookbooks until now. While I know these snails have brought lots of "December dazzle" to fans of my *Cold-Weather Cooking* book, they belong in this collection of Burgundy recipes because they are the best *escargot* creation I know. Indeed, one of my greatest moments of cooking in France came when I received a "two-antennae-up" after daring to serve this slightly Italo-American-ized version of classic *escargots à la bourguignonne,* with its Parmesan cheese, prosciutto, and Pernod, at a feast I was putting on for both my cycling group and an odd collection of scrutinizing French.

In Burgundy, snails are still, more often than not, served stuffed back into their shells and accompanied by special tongs to facil-itate removal for eating. Back on American soil, the notion of unstuffing and stuffing the shells, no matter how aesthetically correct, strikes me as absurdly Sisyphean, so I continue to opt for providing a shelter of prosciutto rather than shell for these endearingly edible little creatures. All of this is not to say, how-ever, that this butter-rich recipe shouldn't be employed by culi-nary masochists, nostalgists, and plain old Francophiles bent on

13

serving snails "shell-locked," as they were first intended to be.

Leftover *escargot* butter has lots of delectable uses. It certainly perks up simple steamed vegetables, but I think my favorite use or "use-up" is to tuck a nugget of the garlicky herb butter into the center of a hamburger before cooking, so that it melts and oozes into the beef during grilling to create a burger that rivals the famous one served at New York's 21 Club.

1 cup (2 sticks) unsalted butter, at room temperature
3 large cloves garlic, minced
2 shallots, minced
½ cup minced fresh parsley, plus additional for garnish
½ cup freshly grated Parmesan cheese
1 tablespoon dry vermouth
1 tablespoon Pernod or other anise liqueur
1 tablespoon fresh lemon juice
½ teaspoon sea or coarse salt
1 teaspoon freshly ground black pepper
36 paper-thin snail-wide strips prosciutto (about
    1 pound)
36 canned Burgundy snails, rinsed, soaked (see Note),
    and drained
Sliced fresh French bread

14

1. Using an electric hand mixer, beat the butter until light and fluffy. Beat in the garlic, shallots, ½ cup parsley, and Parmesan. On low speed, blend in the vermouth, Pernod, and lemon juice. Season with salt and pepper.

2. Spread each slice of prosciutto with a generous smear of the garlic butter. Place a snail at one end of each buttered slice and coil the meat tightly around each snail. Arrange the wrapped snails close together and seam side down in a baking dish or individual gratin dishes—allow 6 per serving. (The snails may be prepared to this point up to 1 day in advance.)

3. When ready to cook the snails, preheat the oven to 400°F.

4. Bake the snails for 10 minutes. Then turn on the broiler and broil the dish a few inches from the heat until the butter is sizzling, 1 to 2 minutes. Sprinkle with a smattering of fresh parsley, insert a toothpick in each snail if serving from a platter, and serve at once with plenty of bread to soak up all the extra garlic butter.

SERVES 12 TO 18 AS A FINGER-FOOD HORS D'OEUVRE OR 6 AS A FIRST COURSE

Note: In order to ensure that canned *escargots* do not have a faint metallic taste from their packing tins, take the following preliminary steps: Place the *escargots* in a colander and rinse under cold water for 3 to 4 minutes. Transfer to a small bowl and cover with fresh cold water to which 3 tablespoons brandy or white wine have been added. Let stand for at least 1 hour. Drain and use as directed in the recipe.

15

Tarte aux Escargots de Chantal

∽

I could not have had a better neighbor than Chantal Leroux during the March I spent in Beaune researching many of my Burgundy recipes. Chantal used to run a flower shop in town, and she kept both her home and my little cottage surrounded by fragrant herbs and beautiful flowers. She was also wonderfully Burgundian in that she gathered *escargots* in nearby vineyards and often concocted batches of delicious home-brewed cassis. Always game for culinary adventure, she shared many insider's tips with me and made invaluable introductions.

When Chantal wasn't able to help me, her sons could, and I am especially grateful for the winery tours they arranged for me in Pommard at Clos des Epeneaux and Domaine Guy Roulot, in Meursault. I can think of no better match for Chantal's earthy tart than a bottle of Guy Roulot Meursault.

PASTRY CRUST
12 tablespoons (1½ sticks) chilled unsalted butter, cut into
    small pieces
1¾ cups unbleached all-purpose flour
Pinch of sea or coarse salt
1 large egg, lightly beaten
2 tablespoons ice water

ESCARGOT FILLING
2 tablespoons unsalted butter
36 canned Burgundy snails, rinsed, soaked (see Note, page 15),
    and drained
3 shallots, minced
12 cloves garlic, minced
¼ cup dry white wine or vermouth
1 cup minced fresh parsley
1½ tablespoons imported Dijon mustard
5 large eggs
1¾ cups heavy (or whipping) cream
¼ teaspoon freshly grated nutmeg
Sea or coarse salt and freshly ground black pepper to taste

1. Make the pastry crust: Place the butter, flour, and salt in a food processor. Process until the mixture resembles coarse meal. Add the egg and the ice water; process until the pastry begins to form a ball. Shape the pastry into a flat disk, wrap in plastic, and refrigerate for at least 1 hour.

2. Preheat the oven to 400°F.

3. Make the filling: Melt the butter over medium heat in a large skillet. Add the snails and sauté until hot and just beginning to crisp, 4 to 5 minutes. Add the shallots and garlic and continue sautéing until softened, 3 to 4 minutes. Add the wine and cook 2 minutes longer. Stir in the parsley and remove from the heat.

17

4. On a lightly floured surface, roll the pastry out into a circle 13 to 14 inches in diameter. Ease the pastry into a 12-inch tart pan; trim and crimp the edges decoratively. Spread the mustard thinly and evenly over the bottom of the pastry shell. Spread the snail mixture evenly on top.

5. Beat the eggs and cream together until well blended. Season with the nutmeg, salt, and pepper. Pour the mixture into the tart shell.

6. Bake the tart until the crust is golden brown and the filling is puffed and set, 30 to 40 minutes. Serve the tart hot, cut into wedges.

MAKES 8 TO 10 SERVINGS

SLOW DOWN, YOU EAT TOO FAST

*B*utterfield & Robinson promotes its biking and walking tours with the slogan "Slow down, you move too fast." The same concept could well be adapted to advertise dining out in Burgundian restaurants. My experience has proven that there must be a conspiracy to keep diners at the table, be it lunch- or dinnertime, for a minimum of three hours. I should have anticipated as much in a region whose favorite author, Henri Vincenot, wrote a beloved book entitled *Le Pape des escargots* (The Pope of the Snails), wherein he coined the phrase *civilisation lente* (civilization of slowness) in reference to Burgundy. The local hot-air balloon company of choice is called Air *Escargot,* and, perhaps, a travel writer put Burgundy in perspective best when he said, "The snail is not just eaten here, it is emulated."

One day, when I was particularly pressed to grab a quick lunch, I stopped into a popular local bistro by the name of Chez Jeanette, in Fixin. I had selected the place because it had posted outside the entrance a "TGV menu," with a picture of France's high-speed train next to it. If memory serves me correctly, the *prix fixe* offering consisted of *pâté de campagne, coq au vin,* a salad, and a simple dessert. When, two and a half hours later, I was still waiting for *l'addition* (the bill), I couldn't help being amused that my "quick" meal had lasted longer than the TGV train ride from Paris to Burgundy.

Savory Pork and Chestnut Patties

Even if you have never traveled to Burgundy, a mere glance at the recipes in this book would be enough to reveal to you that pork and its by-products are a major cornerstone of Burgundian cooking. In fact, whenever I'm feeling overloaded by the never-ending barrage of foods-to-fear that the North American media relishes in reporting on, I delight in seeking comic relief by browsing through Burgundian cookbooks, many of which unabashedly begin with recipes for *soupe au lard* or *brioche aux grattons* (egg- and butter-rich dough studded with crispy fried pieces of pork or duck fat).

The savory patties featured here, known as *crepinettes* in Burgundy, are a fairly typical hors d'oeuvre, though I make mine considerably less fatty than the traditional recipes. The minced chestnuts make for an interesting combination with the ground pork and remind me of favored flavors that go into my Thanksgiving turkey stuffing. Peeled cooked chestnuts are available canned in specialty food stores, if you don't wish to go through the labor of peeling your own.

The patties are delicious sautéed crisp and served warm. Since they are a three-or-four-bite hors d'oeuvre, little plates and forks may be in order. Sometimes I slice the leftovers cold and serve them like pâté with a dab of sharp Dijon mustard on rounds of French bread.

1 pound lean ground pork
½ pound peeled cooked chestnuts, minced
2 shallots, minced
⅓ cup minced fresh parsley
1 teaspoon ground coriander
¾ teaspoon sea or coarse salt
¾ teaspoon freshly ground black pepper
1 large egg
1½ tablespoons marc de Bourgogne or brandy
8 slices bacon
1 tablespoon unsalted butter
1 tablespoon vegetable oil

1. Place the pork and chestnuts together in a food processor and process until well combined. Add the shallots, parsley, coriander, salt, and pepper and process to incorporate. Transfer the mixture to a mixing bowl. In a small bowl, beat the egg and *marc* together and then knead the mixture into the pork to moisten and bind.

2. Cut the bacon strips in half horizontally and then cut each strip in half again lengthwise. Form the pork mixture into 16 balls about the size of a small egg and then flatten them between your palms to make squat patties. Cross two strips of bacon over each patty to form an X on the top, wrapping the ends under the patty to form another X on the bottom. Press gently to make the bacon adhere to the patties.

3. Heat the butter and oil together in a large skillet over medium-high heat. Sauté the patties, in batches if necessary, until browned and crisped on each side and thoroughly cooked through the center, about 15 minutes total cooking time. Transfer the patties to a plate lined with paper towels to drain. Then, arrange on a serving platter or individual plates and serve hot or warm.

MAKES 16 PATTIES (8 SERVINGS)

Warm Chicken Liver Mousse with Crayfish Cream

∽

I t is not surprising that in a region that insists on an *appellation contrôlée* to guarantee the authenticity of its plump and prized Bresse chickens there should also be found a few divine chicken liver recipes. One of the best—*gâteau de foies de volaille*—comes from Restaurant Lea in Montrevel-en-Bresse, and I'm delighted to be able to include it in this book because it epitomizes classic Burgundian cooking.

The newcomer to Burgundy might find the combination of crayfish and chicken livers a bit strange, but Burgundians have long been fond of combining their freshwater crayfish with meat, and the results are delicious and unique. I made my crayfish cream—also known as *sauce Nantua*—with whole, cooked, and frozen crayfish I found in the freezer section of my local supermarket. There are also several mail-order sources in New Orleans for these bright red crustaceans, which are called crawfish there. Fisherman's Cove (800-443-3474) is one that's been recommended to me.

The warm chicken liver mousse is usually served as a first course in Burgundy, but it would also make a sophisticated luncheon entrée. A top-of-the-line white Bur-

21

gundy, such as Corton-Charlemagne, Meursault, or Montrachet, is just the beverage to gild the lily.

CRAYFISH CREAM
1 pound whole crayfish, cooked or uncooked, thawed if frozen
4 tablespoons (½ stick) unsalted butter
3 shallots, minced
¼ pound white mushrooms, wiped clean of any dirt and
    minced
¼ cup brandy
½ cup dry white wine
1½ cups fish stock or bottled clam juice
2½ cups heavy (or whipping) cream
2 tablespoons tomato paste
2 teaspoons dried tarragon
Pinch of cayenne pepper
Sea or coarse salt and freshly ground black pepper to taste

CHICKEN LIVER MOUSSE
2 tablespoons unsalted butter
1 clove garlic, minced
¾ pound chicken livers
2 large eggs and 2 egg yolks
1 cup crème fraîche
1½ teaspoons sea or coarse salt
1 teaspoon freshly ground black pepper
¼ teaspoon freshly grated nutmeg
2 tablespoons minced fresh parsley

1. To make the crayfish cream, remove the tail meat from the crayfish, devein it, and set it aside. Save all of the shells from both the bodies and tails.

2. Melt the butter over medium-high heat in a large skillet; add the shallots and mushrooms and sauté for 5 minutes. Add the crayfish shells and cook 2 minutes more, stirring to coat them with the butter and vegetables. Add the brandy and remove the skillet from the heat. Standing back, carefully ignite the brandy with a long kitchen match, and let it burn until the flames burn out.

3. Add the wine and fish stock to the skillet, bring to a boil over medium-high heat, and cook until the liquid is reduced by half, 10 to 15 minutes. Add the cream and tomato paste, stirring until blended. Season with the tarragon and cayenne. Bring the liquid to a boil again and continue cooking until it is again reduced by half, about 20 minutes.

4. Strain the cream through a sieve into a clean, medium-size saucepan; discard the solids. Stir in the reserved meat from the crayfish tails. If the crayfish are already cooked, just stir over medium heat to reheat; if raw, cook for an additional 2 minutes. Season the sauce with salt and pepper to taste. If not using the sauce immediately, store it in the refrigerator until ready to use. Reheat gently over medium-low heat until hot when ready to use.

23

5. To make the chicken liver mousse, preheat the oven to 375°F. Generously butter six 1-cup ramekins and sprinkle a little minced garlic over the bottom of each. Set aside.

6. Remove any veins from the chicken livers, cut them into

small pieces, and place in a food processor. Process to purée the livers; add the eggs and process until smooth; add the crème fraîche and process again until smooth. Season the purée with the salt, pepper, nutmeg, and parsley. Pour the mousse into the prepared ramekins, filling each about three-quarters full. Arrange the ramekins in a baking pan and add water to the baking pan to come halfway up the sides of the ramekins. Bake the mousses until a toothpick inserted in the center comes out clean, about 30 minutes.

7. Using pot holders, carefully unmold the mousses by inverting them onto individual serving plates. Pool the crayfish cream over and around the mousses. Serve at once.

MAKES 6 SERVINGS

A FEW GOOD
SOUPS &
BREADS

Mushroom Soup

While a decent French *baguette* has become one of those commodities that are increasingly easy to come by in many parts of the world, finding many soups on menus in Burgundy restaurants is a rarity these days. I can only wager that the reasons for this are ones of fickle food fashion—soup must seem too peasanty for the *haute* regional cuisine that many restaurants like to promote. I am nonetheless convinced that soups, and very good ones, must be simmering on the stoves of all those *vignerons'* neat-as-a-pin stone homes we cycle by on our daily biking routes. Such infuriating proximity makes us soup-starved cyclists all the more appreciative of the odd bowl unearthed in a local restaurant. After all, what is a trip to France without at least one crock of bubbling Onion Soup Gratinée?

Bread is, of course, the staff of life, and a *baguette* is usually the staff found strapped to the back rack of my group's bicycles. Once the cycling vacation has ended, however, it is the yen for Burgundy's toasted walnut bread or *pain d'epices* that is likely to drive one into the kitchen with bowl, board, and loaf pan.

Homemade Beef Stock

Many of the wonderfully rich sauces for which the French are justly famous rely on full-bodied, aromatic broth bases distilled from chicken, veal, beef, or fish. It therefore seems only appropriate that the French term *fonds* and English equivalent *stock* double as both culinary and banking terms. *Fonds* means "treasury" in the world of French finance, and it was none other than Julia Child in her original guise of French chef who taught aspiring American epicures to look upon homemade stocks as the "foundation and working capital of the kitchen."

While making any sort of stock from scratch is always a time investment with good gastronomic returns, I bank foremost on this heady beef stock recipe for most of my Burgundian cooking.

27

3 to 4 pounds raw, meaty beef bones, cut into 3- to
    4-inch chunks
1 large onion, coarsely chopped (about 1 cup)
2 large carrots, coarsely chopped (about 1 cup)
3 ribs celery, coarsely chopped (about 1 cup)
2 cups dry red or white wine
4 to 5 quarts cold water
Several sprigs fresh parsley
Several sprigs fresh thyme, or 2 teaspoons dried thyme
3 whole cloves
12 black peppercorns
3 cloves unpeeled garlic, smashed
3 tablespoons tomato paste
Sea or coarse salt to taste

1. Preheat the oven to 450°F.

2. Arrange the beef bones in a single layer in a large flame-proof roasting pan. Sprinkle them with ½ cup each chopped onion, carrot, and celery. Roast, basting frequently with any accumulated pan drippings, until the bones are evenly browned, 35 to 45 minutes.

3. Transfer the bones and vegetables to a large stockpot, discarding any visible melted fat from the pan. Deglaze the roasting pan by pouring in the wine and bringing it to a boil on top of the stove. Stir with a wooden spoon to loosen any browned bits still clinging to the bottom of the pan. Add the deglazed mixture to the stockpot.

4. Add the remaining onion, carrot, and celery to the stockpot along with enough water to cover all the ingredients by 2 inches. Stir in the parsley, thyme, cloves, peppercorns, garlic, and tomato paste. Bring all to a simmer over medium-high heat, skimming off and discarding any scum that floats to the top during the first 15 to 20 minutes of cooking.

5. Continue simmering the stock, uncovered, stirring occasionally, for at least 4 hours. If the liquid evaporates below the top of the stock ingredients, add enough water to cover again.

6. Strain the stock through a large sieve set over a large bowl or clean pot, taking care to extract all the concentrated flavors from the vegetables by pressing them hard against the sieve with the back of a wooden spoon. Discard the solids. Season the strained broth with salt.

7. To degrease the stock, chill it for several hours until the fat hardens on the surface. Skim off and discard the fat. The stock is now ready for use in soups, stews, and sauces. It may also be reheated and boiled down to reduce it further for use in recipes where a more concentrated beef flavor is required. The stock will keep in the refrigerator for 3 days, or it may be frozen in pint or quart containers for up to 3 months.

MAKES ABOUT 3 QUARTS

French Onion Soup Gratinée

29

P atience is a virtue, not only in life, but more specifically in the making of a veritable French onion soup. Throughout my years of cookbook writing, I have had occasion to devise many variations of this Burgundian/Lyonnais classic and must here confess to feeling the utmost satisfaction in finally mustering the discipline to master making the "mother onion soup" of all my previous inventions.

I say *discipline,* not to scare off would-be soup simmerers, but to stress the absolute necessity of making your own beef stock from scratch to serve as the broth base of this otherwise simple soup. Just as I would wish that European diesel trucks may never cross your cycling path while you're pedaling lazily through the splendid vineyards of Puligny-Montrachet or

Gevrey-Chambertin, may brand-name broths like College Inn or Swanson never cross your lips when you're contemplating this recipe.

Nursing your own homemade stock will make you feel like a culinarily correct person and will aromatize your kitchen, clothing, and soul. Once your stock is made, you'll need to spend time minding the sliced onions, which require tender-loving sautéing. For it is only the watched, perfectly wilted, and slightly sugared onion that will caramelize properly. Once your beef stock and golden, well-tended onions are finally combined, generous splashes of vermouth and Cognac are needed to fortify the soup (and perhaps its maker) through another 45 minutes or more of simmering.

The soup should now be ready to receive its *pièce de résistance* (which is really why anyone goes to all this fuss in the first place)—the topping of thickly sliced, garlicky slabs of toasted French bread mounded with a blizzard of freshly and finely shredded Gruyère cheese. For good measure at this point, I am inclined

to add an extra splash of Cognac and smattering of minced raw scallions to each serving before a final meltdown underneath the broiler.

This is the sort of soup from which meals and memories are made. I know because, alas, many of the cyclists on my Burgundy tours have been known to seek respite from the multicourse, Michelin-starred fare of Lameloise and the Hostellerie de Levernois by making an evening's meal of a bowl of *soupe à l'oignon gratinée* at a nearby bistro, Le Gourmandin, in Beaune's central place Carnot.

3 tablespoons unsalted butter

2 tablespoons olive oil

3 pounds (4 to 5 large) yellow or white onions,
   thinly sliced into rings

2 teaspoons sugar

2 tablespoons unbleached all-purpose flour

3 quarts Homemade Beef Stock (page 27)

½ cup dry white vermouth

½ cup Cognac or brandy

Sea or coarse salt and freshly ground black pepper to taste

GRUYÈRE TOASTS AND FINISHING:

⅓ cup olive oil

1 large clove garlic, minced

8 slices French bread (1 inch thick) from a fat loaf

3 to 4 tablespoons Cognac or brandy

1 bunch scallions, trimmed and minced

½ to ¾ pound freshly grated French or
   Swiss Gruyère cheese

1. Heat the butter and olive oil together in a large stockpot over medium-high heat. Add the onions and sauté, stirring frequently, until softened, 5 to 7 minutes. Turn the heat down to low, cover the pot, and cook the onions slowly until soft and translucent, about 15 minutes.

2. Uncover the pot, sprinkle the onions with the sugar, raise the heat to medium-high, and cook the onions, stirring frequently, until they have turned a caramel golden brown color, 25 to 30 minutes.

3. Sprinkle the onions with the flour and cook, stirring constantly, to lightly brown (but not burn) the flour, 2 to 3 minutes. Slowly stir in a cup or so of the beef stock and continue

··

THE CRYING GAME

P eople are always asking me which old wives' tale I subscribe to when it comes to keeping my eyes from tearing while chopping onions. Truth be told, I have only happened upon one surefire way not to have a good cry over the onion family, and that is by wearing contact lenses when chopping. Now, I still cry over spilled milk, beet juice, tomato sauce, and other kitchen catastrophes, but with my vibrantly hued contact lenses, I'm dry-eyed when it comes to the prospect of mincing onions.

··

stirring until smooth and thickened. Gradually add the rest of the beef stock to the pot, then add the vermouth and Cognac.

4. Let the soup simmer, uncovered, over medium heat for at least another 45 minutes or up to 1½ hours more. At the end of 45 minutes, your soup will be good, but if allowed to simmer longer, it will taste richer. Season the soup to taste with salt and freshly ground pepper.

5. Meanwhile, make the French bread *croûtes*: Preheat the oven to 400°F.

6. Combine the garlic and olive oil in a small bowl. Lightly brush one side of each slice of bread all over with the olive oil and arrange, oiled side up, on a baking sheet. Bake the bread slices until light golden brown on top, 10 to 12 minutes.

7. When ready to serve the onion soup, preheat the broiler and place the oven rack 4 to 5 inches from the heat.

8. Ladle 8 large ovenproof earthenware soup bowls three-quarters full with the hot onion soup. Float a French bread *croûte* in the center of each bowl and sprinkle with a little Cognac and 2 table-

spoons of the minced scallions. Generously cover the top of each serving with ½ cup or more of the shredded Gruyère.

9. Arrange the soup bowls on a tray and place underneath the broiler. Cook until the cheese is melted, bubbly, and just beginning to brown, 4 to 5 minutes. Serve at once.

MAKES 8 AMPLE SERVINGS

Mushroom Soup to Excite the Palate

O ne of the grand rewards of huffing and puffing through some of the hillier biking that skirts the Côte d'Or is that you actually feel as if you've earned the privilege of enjoying every single extraordinary mouthful of the *menu gastronomique* at the three-star Restaurant Lameloise in Chagny. Which is exactly what I did recently with a dozen of my fellow cyclists. Gathered around one long celebratory table in a private dining room of this fifteenth-century Burgundian home-turned-restaurant, we ensconced ourselves for five luxurious hours, in chairs as overstuffed as we would soon become. As belts were loosened and the last speck of room possible was made for the final cocoa dusted truffles and paper-thin almond *tuiles,* we all agreed that the dish we would most like to try to recreate back home was the luscious essence of mushroom soup that had been served as our palate cleanser.

When I returned to the restaurant months later to inquire about the recipe, it was graciously and immediately jotted down

33

in the kitchen by master chef Jacques Lameloise himself, while in the midst of lunch service. No wonder the food writer Patricia Wells calls this Burgundy *cuisinier* "perhaps the most easygoing and modest grand chef in France."

The soup couldn't be simpler. Basic white mushrooms, milk, cream, and chicken stock are simmered slowly and then puréed to silky smoothness. Because vegetables grown in North America don't seem to have the same concentration of flavor as those grown in France, I have insured an intense mushroom flavor in this transplanted version of the Lameloise original by bolstering the common mushrooms with a few dried cèpes, warmed and reconstituted in white wine. "Spirited" cook that I am, I also couldn't resist the embellishment of a whisper of Cognac as a seemingly natural complement to the earthiness of the mushrooms.

At Lameloise, the soup is served very elegantly in miniature, silver-plated tureens. At home I try to follow formal suit by using my most delicate china bowls, though I am more inclined to serve this mushroom distillation as a first course rather than a creamy segue in the middle of multicourse plenty.

34

½ ounce dried cèpes
1 cup dry white wine
2 tablespoons unsalted butter
1 pound white mushrooms, wiped clean of any dirt
*   and coarsely chopped*
2 cups milk
2 cups heavy (or whipping) cream
4 cups chicken stock, preferably homemade
Salt and freshly ground white pepper to taste
2 tablespoons Cognac (optional)
Snipped fresh chives for garnish

1. Combine the dried cèpes and white wine in a small saucepan and bring to a boil over medium-high heat. Simmer for 5 minutes, remove from the heat, and let stand for 15 minutes. Strain the liquid from the mushrooms through a fine mesh sieve and reserve. Coarsely chop the cèpes and reserve as well.

2. Melt the butter over medium heat in a large stockpot. Add the chopped white mushrooms and sauté until they begin to exude their juices, about 5 minutes. Add the cèpes, reserved broth, milk, and cream and bring to a boil, stirring occasionally. Lower the heat and simmer the soup, uncovered, stirring every now and then, for 45 minutes.

3. Purée the hot soup in a blender in batches until very smooth. Return the soup to a large clean pot and thin by stirring in the chicken stock. Season with salt and white pepper and stir in the Cognac. Warm the soup over low heat until heated through, about 10 minutes. Ladle small portions of the soup into your finest bowls and garnish each portion with a sprinkling of chives. Serve at once.

MAKES 8 SERVINGS

35

Everyday French Vegetable Soup

I t is unfortunate that hearty soups are not currently in vogue in Burgundy's restaurants, because they are just the sort of fare that many cyclists on my trips crave in cooler weather as a quick lunchtime pick-me-up. The odd person who finds himself or herself separated from bicycling buddies at noontime out in the restaurantless countryside might just be lucky enough, however, to be invited into a farmer's kitchen and served a soul-satisfying *potage ménagère* similar to the recipe here.

4 tablespoons (½ stick) unsalted butter
4 leeks, trimmed, washed, and minced
3 cloves garlic, minced
1 bulb fennel or 3 ribs celery, trimmed and minced
1 teaspoon dried thyme
3 large carrots, peeled and cut into ¼-inch-thick coins
1 large turnip (about 1 pound), peeled and cut into ½-inch chunks
4 cups shredded green cabbage
2 medium potatoes, peeled and thinly sliced
2 cups canned or cooked dried white beans, drained
11 cups chicken stock, preferably homemade
1 cup white Burgundy wine or domestic chardonnay
1 bay leaf
Sea or coarse salt and freshly ground black pepper to taste
Minced fresh parsley for garnish

1. Melt the butter in a large pot over medium heat. Add the leeks, garlic, fennel, and thyme; sauté until very soft, about 15 minutes. Add the carrots, turnip, cabbage, potatoes, and beans. Pour in the chicken stock and wine and season with the bay leaf, salt, and pepper. Let the soup simmer, uncovered, until all the vegetables are tender, 35 to 45 minutes.

2. Ladle the soup into large soup bowls and garnish each serving with a smattering of fresh parsley.

MAKES 8 SERVINGS

GINGERBREAD ABROAD

Besides being a center for the best mustard and cassis, the city of Dijon is also known gastronomically for its *pain d'épices*—a European version of what Americans call gingerbread. Bread made with honey dates back to ancient Greeks and Romans, but it was not until the Middle Ages that spices were added along with the honey to create a sweet spice bread. This type of bread was brought to Dijon via Flanders, and it became very popular with the dukes of Burgundy. During the seventeenth century, the perfected recipe was officially named *pain d'épices,* and its renown, associated with the city of Dijon, began to spread far and wide. Alexandre Dumas noted in his grand dictionary of cuisine that *pain d'épices* excites the appetite, quenches thirst, and aids in digestion.

One of the best places to sample *pain d'épices* in Burgundy is at the quaint Mulot et Petitjean shop in Dijon, where the spiced bread is baked in different shapes and flavors, according to season. For me, *pain d'épices* was not a matter of love at first bite, but I found myself haunted by its flavor in the wonderful way that a taste can become distinctly associated with a place. One day, I helped myself to a slice of *pain d'épices* proffered by the front desk at the Château de Gilly, in Vougeot. Hours later, as I was pedaling about on my bicycle without a lunch spot in sight, I began to nibble at the bread—it hit the spot so perfectly that I became a devotee from that moment on. For the recipe, see page 38.

Pain d'Épices

This recipe is adapted from the one kindly jotted down for me at the Château de Gilly (see box, page 37). *Chez moi*, I've become fond of having the bread for breakfast with *café au lait* in an elegant oversize cup that I brought home from a favorite tableware shop in Beaune. I find it quite the Proustian experience, as the savor of the spices never fails to evoke rich memories of my travels through Burgundy.

Butter and flour for preparing the pan
3¾ cups unbleached all-purpose flour
1 cup sugar
2 teaspoons baking powder
½ teaspoon salt
1 tablespoon ground ginger
1½ teaspoons ground cinnamon
1 teaspoon ground coriander
1 teaspoon anise seeds
¼ teaspoon ground nutmeg
¼ teaspoon ground cloves
2 large eggs, lightly beaten
¾ cup honey
1 cup warm water
⅓ cup dark or amber rum

1. Preheat the oven to 400°F. Butter and lightly flour a 9 x 5-inch loaf pan.

2. In a large mixing bowl, stir together the flour, sugar, baking powder, salt, and all of the spices. Make a well in the cen-

38

ter of the combined dry ingredients. In a small bowl, whisk together the eggs, honey, water, and 2 tablespoons of the rum. Pour the liquids into the well, and stir with a sturdy wooden spoon until thoroughly combined with the dry ingredients to make a smooth but thick batter. Spread the batter evenly into the prepared pan.

3. Bake the bread for 15 minutes and then reduce the temperature to 325°F. Continue baking until a toothpick inserted in the center of the loaf comes out clean, 40 to 45 minutes more. Turn the bread out onto a rack to cool. As the bread is cooling, brush it lightly all over with the remaining rum, so that it is absorbed by the warm bread. When ready to serve, cut the bread into ½-inch slices. The bread lasts at least 1 week, well wrapped in plastic wrap.

MAKES ONE 9 X 5-INCH LOAF

39

Toasted Walnut Bread

If I had to pinpoint what I live for most when traveling in Burgundy, it would be the wine, first, and the perfectly ripened cheeses, second. Better yet, the wine and cheeses together! The cheese course in the best Burgundian restaurants is always accompanied by thinly sliced walnut bread, rather than everyday *baguettes*.

TAKING TIME TO SMELL
THE EPOISSES

D escribing Burgundy's Epoisses cheese as pungent is an understatement. So ripened is this rich, runny raw cow's-milk cheese, aged slowly in a daily bath of alcoholic *marc de Bourgogne,* that it has never been exported. The locals speak the truth when they joke "it's the cheese you smell from farthest away!"

Yet Epoisses is precisely the sort of regional specialty that should be discovered and savored while meandering by bicycle through the Burgundy countryside. Since I not only love but crave the cheese, I make a point of serving it at all the Burgundian bicycling picnics I stage and always select it first off the cheese cart at restaurants. Not everyone in my groups, however, is as enthusiastic about Epoisses as I am. In fact, I'll never forget the handsome and fastidious fellow from Southern California who hurled his first sampling of Epoisses over the cliff by our panoramic picnic site. The poor chap proceeded to sniff his fingertips for the rest of the trip, swearing the awful odor of the cheese never dissipated. I seem to recall that a few of his more good-humored traveling companions sneaked a round of Epoisses into his suitcase for further aging on his twelve-hour flight back to the West Coast.

Fortunately, Burgundy is home to less-aromatic cheeses. Two of them are crafted appropriately by mild-mannered monks— Pierre-Qui-Vire, made by Benedictine monks deep in the Morvan forest, and Cîteaux, produced by Cistercian monks at their abbey not far from the Côte de Nuits vineyards. Ami du Chambertin and Saint-Florentin are two other fine regional cheeses to sample.

I like to follow suit at home whenever I'm feeling an extra-strong yearning for the magic of the Côte d'Or.

The *marc*-soaked raisins in the bread are optional. The bread is moister when made with the raisins, but crunchier without them. Take your pick.

> 1 package (¼ ounce) active dry yeast
> 1¾ cups warm water
> 1½ tablespoons honey
> ¼ cup walnut oil
> 2 teaspoons sea or coarse salt
> 1 cup whole-wheat flour
> 3½ to 4½ cups bread flour
> ½ cup golden raisins, plumped for at least 1 hour in
>   ¼ cup marc de Bourgogne or brandy (optional)
> 1½ cups lightly toasted walnuts (page 72), coarsely chopped
> 1 large egg beaten with 1 tablespoon water, for glazing

1. In a large bowl, combine the yeast and water and let stand until foamy, about 5 minutes. Stir in the honey, walnut oil, and salt. Stir in the whole-wheat flour and then gradually work in enough of the bread flour to form a workable, semi-stiff dough. Turn out onto a lightly floured surface and knead until smooth and satiny, 6 to 8 minutes. Transfer the dough to a large, clean bowl; cover with plastic wrap or a clean kitchen towel and let rise in a warm place until doubled in bulk, 1 to 1½ hours.

2. Punch down the dough and turn out onto a lightly floured surface. Knead in the raisins, if using, and the walnuts. Divide the dough in half and roll each half into a classic *baguette* shape. Transfer to 2 parchment-lined baking sheets and let rise, uncovered, in a warm place for 30 minutes.

3. Preheat the oven to 375°F.

4. Brush the *baguettes* with the beaten egg mixture. Using a sharp knife or a razor, make 4 or 5 diagonal gashes at intervals over the top of each *baguette*. Bake until the loaves are nicely browned and sound hollow when tapped lightly on the undersides, 35 to 45 minutes. Transfer the loaves to racks and let them cool completely.

MAKES 2 BAGUETTES

A DAY IN THE LIFE OF A
BURGUNDY
BIKE TOUR

Tolstoy once penned that "all happy families are alike," but I have personally found that even though all the bicycle tours I lead are happy ones, no two are ever similar. While it is true that much of the allure of seeing small pockets of Europe by bicycle comes from feeling reconnected to a time-honored, more agriculturally governed, slower-paced way of life, the mix of people within a group (including the guides); the seasons; weather; newly discovered hotels, restaurants, routes, and even celestial forces, if you will, conspire to make every weeklong cycling adventure unique.

What may seem typical to a veteran guide may well be extraordinary for a newcomer to the experience of seeing Europe by bicycle. For the purpose of offering a bit of insight, I here recount the second day of a Burgundy bicycle tour I recently guided:

The average age in this particular group was younger than most, as many were friends from California traveling together in celebration of the fortieth birthdays of a smattering of the husbands. The warm-up ride through the most prestigious white wine vineyards in Burgundy—and the world for that matter—was high-spirited, with several sliding easily into the wine-drenched life of the region by buying and shipping home cases of Puligny-Montrachet and Chassagne-Montrachet from the sleepy little tasting *caveau* in Chassagne-Montrachet, obviously the perfect rest stop for the group at hand.

The collective energy was unusually adrenergic, and a few members of the group went jogging immediately after our 15-kilometer (10 mile) warm-up ride—a first in my guiding experience! Everybody seemed to appreciate the easy feeling of the Hôtel le Montrachet, and the sensational individual warm apple tarts served for dessert (see page 172) put all in a fine mood to continue the revelry over fiery *marc de Bourgogne* nightcaps in the hotel's cozy bar. Fortunately for us, our host, *hôtelier* Thierry Gazagnes, was more humored than he was disgruntled by our ongoing celebration.

The next morning I was amazed to see fresh enthusiasm and no hangovers at our 8 o'clock *petit déjeuner.* I didn't know whether to attribute this to sublime wine, beautiful biking, strong French coffee, buttery croissants, or youth. The upcoming ride would be 50 kilometers (32 to 33 miles) through rolling hills, more vineyards, and quiet farmlands in the Côte Chalonnaise. Normally, one guide cycles with the group and the other sweeps the route, driving the luggage van and offering rides to the fatigued. However, my co-guide and I had so much confidence in this group that we decided we would both bicycle and truly enjoy what was sure to be a beautiful October day on the road. After a few minor mechanical adjustments to the bikes, everybody was en route between 9:30 and 10 A.M.

The first few route instructions took us over the now familiar vineyards surrounding Puligny-Montrachet and into Santenay. After a while, the vineyards gave way to stream- and cow-flecked farmlands. I encouraged a slight detour to refill water bottles in the little village of Chamilly. There is an ancient pump in the center of town that has been a watering stop for horses for hundreds of years. I like the thought of water having a history as rich as the region's wines.

Our group of twenty-five dispersed into congenial little clusters of cyclists. The roads were quiet and rural enough to allow biking and chatting abreast without fear of notoriously crazed European drivers. The wine town of Mercurey was the day's halfway point, and I offered to show the handful of people I biked with how enjoyable a bit of local wine tasting could be in these less famous Burgundy vineyards. After a good morning's biking and a few comparative swishes of red Givry, Mercurey, and Montagny wines, my cycling companions were primed to forget about all the indulgent calories consumed during the previous evening's multi-course feast and actually feel deserving of lunch.

Puligny-Montrachet

Chassagne-Montrachet

Santenay

Remigny

Rully

Mercurey

Chamilly

DÉGUSTATION DU VIN

We checked out the Michelin-starred Hostellerie du Val d'Or, on the fringes of Mercurey, but found it a mite too fancy for our mood. Not much else appeared to be happening lunch-wise in Mercurey, until my nose for eating establishments led me to the local working-class restaurant at the end of the main commercial street. I negotiated a table for six, and we sat down to the day's offering—lovely leeks vinaigrette and delicious fresh eggs whisked into a simple but satisfying cheese omelet. Now, such a basic French lunch may not make the folks back home envious, but I knew that we had accomplished a rare feat in the spectrum of Burgundian repasts by consuming light fare in just under an hour and a half. We actually felt capable of getting back onto our bikes for an afternoon of leisurely cycling back to the Hôtel le Montrachet.

The afternoon's pedaling up and down through just-harvested vineyards, against the backdrop of a dramatic, partly cloudy autumn sky was pure postcard material—everyone's dream of biking in Burgundy made real. Even I, usually too preoccupied with guiding responsibilities to remember to take pictures, posed, decadently reclined on an ancient stone wall, bicycle in the foreground, with the magnificent Château de Rully looming behind. I remember thinking that this had the potential to become a Christmas card, or better yet, an author photograph for some yet-to-be-written book.

Roughly 5 kilometers away

Mercurey

Château de Rully

from our home port of Puligny-Montrachet, the small group of cyclists I was with ran across the California contingent of the group, who had taken over the only bar in the sleepy village of Remigny. Kronenbourg beers were flowing, along with tales of the fabulous picnic they had orchestrated around an abandoned cart in an open field, which naturally became the postprandial focal point of numerous group photographs. Once again I found myself marveling at how a French beer stop always manages to refresh, bring out camaraderie, prolong an afternoon's fun, and make the last few kilometers of a day's ride seem effortless.

Once back at the Hôtel le Montrachet, the bikes were left to rest overnight in an outbuilding, and naps and hot baths were in order for late-afternoon relaxation. Another great evening, after all, was in store. Our group was to enjoy the extraordinary privilege of having a private wine tasting in the home of the world-renowned wine maker Olivier Leflaive. Monsieur Leflaive conveniently lives a few doors down from the hotel, and we sauntered over to his home at twilight as nonchalantly as we might have dropped in on a friendly neighbor for a chat and cup of coffee.

Côte Chalonnaise Cart Picnic

Already there were those in the group who would have loved to change their name to something as melodic sounding as Olivier Leflaive, and others who instantly contemplated trading a life in investment banking for a life in the seductive world of Burgundy wine making.

Fantasies aside, Olivier was intent on making us grasp how important the location of an individual vineyard in Burgundy is to the finesse of the final product. Our day's biking made it easy to visualize the difference between flat vineyards close to the national highway and those angled higher up on that famous golden slope, for which the Côte d'Or is named. The delicious Leflaive wines that were next poured into our tasting glasses from nearby *Village* and *Premier Cru* vineyards conspired to make this distinction as indelible to the tastebuds as it would become to our visual memories. One insatiably curious fellow in the group became sidetracked by the beauty of the oak barrels for aging wine that line the Leflaive cellars. Olivier mentioned that they were made just up the road in Meursault, and side trips on the next day's cycling route were planned.

A light-headed hour and a half later, it became evident that the only thing that could draw the group from the wonderful Leflaive wine cellar was the prospect of another memorable meal at the Hôtel le Montrachet, accompanied by more Leflaive wine! The hotel's kitchen was closed for the night, but Thierry Gazagnes had offered to barbecue for our group, and the ensuing meal of rosy grilled lamb and spicy merguez sausage was another triumph, perfectly suited to the relaxed ebullience that seemed to have become second nature to the group on that second evening in the heart of rural Burgundy.

FROMAGE ET OEUFS

Cheese Soufflé

Burgundy

Oeufs en Meurette

CHASSAGNE-MONTRACHET ·   MEURSAULT · ECHEVRONNE

When leisurely days are passed pedaling by billowing pastures dotted with Burgundy's famed Charolais cows, sheep, and goats, the connections between the land and its earthy cuisine—a celebration of butter, cheese, and thick cream—are at once understood. Cycle through the aromatic but tiny village of Epoisses, or leave the splendor of the elegant Château de Gilly Hotel, to explore the nearby ruins of the austere Abbaye de Cîteaux, where Cistercian monks still make a luscious, runny cow's milk cheese, and you'll no doubt grasp why so many of the Burgundy's cheeses bearing the same names as these villages and monasteries evoke sheer ecstasy.

Glance beyond Côte d'Or and Beaujolais vineyards to the fertile land of Bresse, famous for its poultry, and stop trying to solve the age-old conundrum of which came first—the chicken or the egg—and instead concentrate on which is more delicious. Can any true Francophile wonder why I should come to ask—Is there anything better than *fromage et oeufs,* or cheese and eggs, in Burgundy?

This may be a short chapter, but the worthiest of recipes come in the littlest of chapters.

Cheese Soufflé from the Hautes Côtes

The European base of operations for our tour groups is in Beaune, and every Friday night a person from company headquarters is designated to come up with an idea to entertain any of the cycling guides who may be in town. One Friday evening at sunset, in the midst of the autumn grape harvest, a group of us ended up wending our way through vineyard after vineyard up into the Hautes Côtes de Beaune, where a spectacular cheese soufflé was timed for our arrival at a little local nameless restaurant. I think the anticipation of the hot, perfectly crusted soufflé enhanced the already extraordinary beauty of our ride, and in homage to the winy wafts of the harvest that pervaded the dusky air of that evening, I have added a little white wine to the base of my soufflé recipe so that it comes close to smelling and tasting like my memories of that indelible evening.

51

The making of a soufflé has long symbolized culinary intimidation, but in truth, it's "as easy as cake"—if you can successfully fold egg whites into a cake batter, you can make this savory counterpart without trembling. The one difference is that a hot soufflé will suffer no excuses of tardiness, which, indeed, is what makes it so ethereally romantic.

In France, a cheese soufflé is usually served as a first course, but *chez moi* it takes center stage at dinner, with the simple yet splendid accompaniments of a crisp green salad, a bottle of white Burgundy at cellar temperature, and a crackling blaze in the fireplace.

3½ tablespoons unsalted butter
2 tablespoons grated Parmesan cheese
2½ tablespoons unbleached all-purpose flour
1 cup half-and-half, scalded and cooled for
   a few minutes
½ cup dry white wine
1 tablespoon imported Dijon mustard
4 large egg yolks, at room temperature
1 cup grated French or Swiss Gruyère cheese
Salt and freshly ground white pepper to taste
6 large egg whites, at room temperature

1. Preheat the oven to 400°F. Butter a 1½-quart soufflé dish with 1 tablespoon of the butter and sprinkle with the Parmesan cheese to coat the inside of the dish lightly all over. (This makes the outside of the soufflé extra crusty.)

2. Melt the remaining 2½ tablespoons butter in a medium-size saucepan over medium heat. Whisk in the flour to make a thick paste, or roux, and continue to cook, stirring constantly, for 2 minutes. The roux should not brown. Gradually whisk in the scalded half-and-half and white wine to make a smooth, thick white sauce. Whisk in the mustard and then the egg yolks, one by one, whisking well after each addition. Remove the mixture from the heat and add the Gruyère cheese, stirring until it is melted. Season this base mixture well with the salt and white pepper, bearing in mind that the taste will be diluted by the egg whites when they are folded in.

3. In a clean bowl, copper if possible, beat the egg whites until stiff but not dry. Gently fold a quarter of the egg whites into the cheese base and then fold the mixture back into the remaining egg whites, whisking as gently as possible to thoroughly combine.

4. Pour the soufflé mixture into the prepared dish and with

52

your index finger, trace a circle around the top of the soufflé 1 inch from the rim of the dish to make a groove that will make the soufflé rise in a cap as it bakes. Bake the soufflé until well puffed and golden, 20 to 25 minutes. Serve immediately.

MAKES 3 TO 4 SERVINGS

....

A SOUFFLÉ IS SOMETHING THAT ISN'T THERE AND TASTES VERY GOOD.

BARBARA GRIZZUTI HARRISON, QUOTING A 3-YEAR-OLD FRIEND

....

53

Oeufs en Meurette

∾

O*eufs en meurette*—poached eggs served in a silky red wine sauce speckled with pearl onions, mushrooms, and crisped bacon—represents Burgundy cooking at its finest. For years I neglected to order them when in Burgundy because to my American sensibilities, poached eggs seemed an incongruous first course in a typically lavish Burgundian dinner. Indeed, order *oeufs en meurette* at the Hostellerie des Clos, in Chablis, and not only will your meal begin with three(!) eggs floating in a very rich sauce but you'll immediately grasp why the famous letter-writing Madame de Sévigné penned that the countryside of Burgundy had air "which you have only to breathe to get fat."

The best *oeufs en meurette* I've ever tasted are served in the splendidly vaulted dining room of the Château de Gilly, an imposing hotel in which cyclists on my Burgundy tour have the luxury of reposing for two nights during their *Route des Grands Crus* bicycling trip. Here, two eggs are served in separate *cocottes*, one napped in the traditional red wine *meurette* and the other in an innovative and equally delicious white wine variation. After a bit of jovial persistence, I succeeded in coaxing the recipe for the red wine version from Gilly's charming manager, J. L. Bottigliero, and it is my adaptation of this recipe that I am pleased to share here. Note: I prefer to serve my *oeufs en meurette* as a brunch dish rather than first course to a meal.

MEURETTE SAUCE

3 cups red Burgundy table wine, preferably with
    13% alcohol
1 cup Homemade Beef Stock (page 27)
2 tablespoons sugar
2 cloves garlic, minced
2 bay leaves
½ teaspoon dried thyme
2 tablespoons unsalted
    butter, at room
    temperature
2 tablespoons unbleached
    all-purpose flour
Sea or coarse salt and
    freshly ground black
    pepper to taste

GARNISHES
24 pearl onions
8 ounces slab bacon, rind removed, cut into ¾-inch dice
Pinch of sugar
2 tablespoons unsalted butter
1 cup thinly sliced white mushrooms

EGGS AND FINISHING THE DISH
3 tablespoons white wine vinegar
8 large eggs
8 rounds white bread (4 inches in diameter), toasted and
    buttered (split English muffins may be substituted)
3 tablespoons minced fresh parsley

1. To make the *meurette* sauce: Combine the wine, beef stock, sugar, garlic, bay leaves, and thyme in a medium-size nonreactive saucepan. Bring the mixture to a boil over medium-high heat and continue to boil gently until the liquid is reduced by half, about 15 minutes. Strain the reduced liquid into a large clean saucepan, discarding the solids. Keep warm over medium-low heat. Using your fingers or a fork, knead together the butter and flour until thoroughly combined, to make what the French call a *beurre manié*. Whisk the *beurre manié* slowly, half-teaspoon by half-teaspoon, into the *meurette* sauce until it is silky and somewhat thickened. Season the sauce with salt and pepper and keep warm over low heat. (The *meurette* sauce may also be made up to 2 days in advance, stored in the refrigerator, and then reheated gently over low heat.)

2. To prepare the garnishes, begin by peeling the pearl onions. Unfortunately, the blanch-and-slip-away-the-skins method does not work well with pearl onions, and it is best to peel them with the aid of a small, sharp paring knife. Set the onions aside.

3. Sauté the bacon in a large skillet over medium-high heat until

crisp. Drain on layers of paper towels and set aside. Pour off all but 2 tablespoons of bacon fat from the skillet. Add the onions to the skillet and sauté them over medium-high heat until they are browned all over, 6 to 8 minutes. Add a pinch of sugar to the skillet and continue sautéing until the onions become lightly caramelized and are tender, 3 to 4 minutes more. Add the onions to the *meurette* sauce.

56

4. Melt the butter over medium heat in a small skillet. Add the mushrooms and sauté them until all their liquid has evaporated and they have become lightly browned. Stir them into the *meurette* sauce.

5. To poach the eggs, bring a large skillet of water to a boil and stir in the vinegar. Carefully break the eggs into the simmering water and poach them to the desired degree of doneness. Have ready 4 large, shallow soup dishes. Place 2 rounds of buttered toast side by side in each dish. Carefully remove the poached eggs from the skillet with a slotted spoon, draining well, and place an egg atop each toast round. Spoon the warm *meurette* sauce generously over and around the eggs. Sprinkle each serving with some of the reserved bacon and a smattering of parsley. Serve immediately.

MAKES 4 SERVINGS

Deviled Eggs Dijonnaise

I believe French cuisine honors the basic egg with more respect than any other world cuisine; a plain yet perfectly boiled egg often stands elevated to a favored first course at rustic country meals. The following somewhat fancier preparation is well on its way to earning post-Easter-egg-hunt hall-of-fame status in my recipe file.

Yolks of hard-cooked eggs take on an extra xanthic hue when mashed with generous amounts of tangy Dijon mustard. A subsequent baking of the restuffed eggs with splashes of wine vinegar and dabs of sweet butter imparts a Burgundian elegance not normally associated with our everyday picnic deviled eggs. Serve these warm eggs as a spring hors d'oeuvre or a splendid garnish to Burgundian roast pork or ham recipes, or go one step further and let them star on their own at the center of a weekend brunch.

57

8 extra-large hard-cooked eggs

2 heaping tablespoons imported Dijon mustard

⅓ cup heavy (or whipping) cream

2 small shallots, minced

1 tablespoon minced fresh parsley

1 tablespoon minced fresh chives

1 tablespoon minced fresh tarragon, or 1 teaspoon
     dried tarragon

Sea or coarse salt and freshly ground black pepper to taste

2 tablespoons unsalted butter, at room temperature

2 tablespoons white wine or champagne vinegar

1. Preheat the oven to 350°F.

2. Peel the hard-cooked eggs and slice them in half lengthwise. Carefully scoop out the yolks and place them in a mixing bowl. Using a fork or electric hand mixer, mash/beat the yolks with the mustard, cream, shallots, and herbs to form a creamy paste. Season to taste with salt and pepper.

3. Spoon the egg yolk mixture into a pastry tube fitted with a star tip. Pipe about 2 tablespoons filling decoratively into the hollow of each half of a cooked egg white and arrange the eggs in a shallow gratin dish just large enough to hold them in a single layer. Dot each egg with a little bit of butter and sprinkle the vinegar over all.

4. Bake the eggs until just beginning to brown, 12 to 15 minutes. Serve at once, at least 2 egg halves per person.

MAKES 6 TO 8 SERVINGS

FABULOUSLY FRENCH
SALADES ET LEGUMES

Asparagus with Aigrelette Sauce

Grilled Mushrooms

Potato Salad Lyonnaise

ARNAY-LE-DUC

BEAUNE

S ome people think of France first in terms of high fashion, splendid art and architecture, or profound intellect. I, too, relish such cerebral delights; but I also think, and sometimes a bit too much, about how the French can bring classic perfection to an all-green salad, a simply steamed potato, or garlicky grilled mushroom.

Burgundy's vegetables, whether hawked daily at Dijon's sprawling covered *halles,* or spilling forth from ramshackle carts crammed into Beaune's Saturday morning market, or simply spied while coasting past the only food store in sleepy little villages like Puligny-Montrachet, St. Romain, or Chambolle-Musigny never fail to elicit admiration. I enthusiastically gather chorus lines of slender carrots, cloudlike heads of cauliflower, lipstick-red radishes, baskets of woodsy mushrooms, and willowy asparagus spears to serve as crudités at the cycling picnics I love to host *en route* and then commit their crisp and earthy essences to memory for creations to be cooked and savored again on familiar home turf.

Simple Green Salad with a Perfected French Vinaigrette

∾

I've never eaten a *salade verte,* or green salad, anywhere in France, regardless of a restaurant's rank, that I didn't adore. It is hard to say whether it should be attributable to all the biking I do in Burgundy's agriculturally bountiful countryside or the fact that I'm in the midst of the region that makes the world's finest mustard, but the salads I eat daily in Burgundy always strike me as the most sublime of all. Burgundians, I surmise, must be born with a whisk in hand, for all seem instinctively to know how to make the vinaigrette of one's dreams from the same basic ingredients: pungent Dijon mustard, vinegar, salt, and oil. Indeed, it was in the Beaunois kitchen of a friend that ten years of questing ended with my learning the little secrets and proportion perfection of all those vinaigrettes I had long admired.

To my palate, the best vinaigrette recipes also include a raw egg yolk, which lends extra creaminess and helps the dressing cling to soft and buttery baby lettuces. If, however, you are not able to buy the most impeccably fresh eggs, and recent health warnings have succeeded in making you fearful of raw egg yolks, then feel free to omit the egg yolk. You'll still end up with a mighty tasty vinaigrette.

This plain salad is embellished in numerous ways in the restaurants we cycle to in Burgundy. At the wonderfully rustic Ferme de Rolle in the sprawling farmlands north of vineyard-dense Nuits-St.-Georges and Gevrey-Chambertin, it is served with *croûtes* of French bread oozing melted *Epoisses* cheese. Many other restaurants place warm chèvre in the middle of the salad.

Whatever your preference, imported Dijon mustard must be used in the vinaigrette to impart the proper signature tang.

VINAIGRETTE
1 large egg yolk (optional)
1 heaping tablespoon imported Dijon mustard
¾ teaspoon sea or coarse salt
3 tablespoons white wine or champagne vinegar
¾ cup vegetable oil
¼ cup olive oil

SALAD
2 medium heads Boston lettuce
2 tablespoons minced fresh parsley or chives
Sea or coarse salt and freshly ground black pepper to taste

1. To make the vinaigrette, whisk the egg yolk (if using), mustard, salt, and vinegar together in a small bowl until smooth. Gradually whisk in the oils to form a creamy emulsion the consistency of a thin mayonnaise. Store the vinaigrette in the refrigerator if not using within the hour. The vinaigrette will keep for approximately 1 week in the refrigerator.

2. To assemble the salad, carefully wash the lettuce, remove the tough lower center ribs, and then dry the leaves in a salad spinner or tea towel. Tear the leaves into large bite-size pieces and place in a large salad bowl. Toss the greens with just enough of the vinaigrette—about ¼ cup—to coat lightly all over. Sprinkle the salad with the minced herbs and season with more salt, if desired, and freshly ground black pepper to taste. Serve at once.

SERVES 6 TO 8

Mixed Baby Lettuces with Warm Cassis Vinaigrette and Foie Gras Toasts

When speaking in terms of regional cooking, *foie gras* is usually associated with southwestern France. Yet every gastronomic temple worthy of its accolades throughout France will feature divinely rich *foie gras*, and restaurants in Burgundy are certainly no exception.

The salad here is designed around two favorite culinary souvenirs that bicyclists and other visitors like to cart back from their travels in France—fabulous cassis from Lucien Jacob in Echevronne, in Burgundy, and tinned or jarred pure duck or goose liver pâté purchased either from weekly open-air markets or at last-minute *gastronomique* kiosks in French airports. Delicious American-made *foie gras* products can also be ordered from the vivacious Ariane Daugin of D'Artagnan in New Jersey (201-729-0748).

Since this rather extravagant salad combines sweet, savory, and rich flavors all at once, wine can be a tough match. I suggest a flute of fine French Champagne or a glass of slightly sweet Alsatian Riesling.

63

WARM CASSIS VINAIGRETTE
½ cup walnut or hazelnut oil
3 shallots, minced
½ cup vegetable oil
2½ tablespoons red wine vinegar
1 tablespoon fresh lemon juice
¼ cup crème de cassis
1 tablespoon honey
Sea or coarse salt and freshly ground black pepper
    to taste

FOIE GRAS TOASTS AND SALAD
6 ounces best-quality terrine or pâté of duck or goose
    foie gras, slightly chilled
12 rounds French bread (½ inch thick), toasted
12 to 14 cups mixed baby lettuces and greens, washed
    and spun dry (see Note)
2 semiripe red-skinned pears, cored and cut into thin slices
⅓ cup hazelnuts, lightly toasted, skinned, and coarsely chopped

1. Make the warm cassis vinaigrette: Heat
¼ cup of the walnut oil in a small saucepan
over medium heat. Add the shallots and sauté
for 5 minutes. Reduce heat to low and whisk
in the remaining ¼ cup walnut oil along with
the vegetable oil, vinegar, lemon juice, cassis, and honey. Season with salt and pepper
to taste. Keep the vinaigrette warm over low
heat while preparing the salad. (The vinaigrette may also be made in advance and
reheated. It will keep in the refrigerator for
at least 1 week.)

2. To make the *foie gras* toasts, spread the *foie gras* generously over each toast round. Set aside in a cool place until ready to use.

3. When ready to serve the salad, heat 6 salad plates, 8 to 9 inches in diameter. Toss the baby lettuces together with the pears in a large mixing bowl and divide this mixture evenly among the 6 warmed plates. Sprinkle the top of each salad with some chopped hazelnuts.

4. Heat the cassis vinaigrette over medium-high heat until it begins to sizzle. Immediately spoon about 2 tablespoons of the vinaigrette over each salad. Place two *foie gras* toasts on the edge of each salad and serve at once.

MAKES 6 SERVINGS

Note: Baby lettuces, or mesclun, are available at specialty food stores and some supermarkets.

65
····

Salade de (Tom) Nevers

A *Salade de Nevers* is a pungent warm salad named after the city of Nevers, the capital of the Nièvre region of Burgundy, located on the wild western fringes of the Morvan forests, far from the vineyard-clad slopes of most Burgundy cycling routes. While Nevers gains culinary credibility from its reputation as a center for the famed Charolais cattle, I felt especially compelled to include this regional specialty because I happen to live in the

wild outskirts of a section of Nantucket Island known as Tom Nevers. While *Nevers* is obviously pronounced differently on Nantucket than in France, the near pun was simply too delicious to resist. Thus, I here present a winning combination of dandelion greens, crisp bacon, strong mustard, and Roquefort cheese destined to become my "house salad" for (n)ever-more.

⅓ pound slab bacon, rind
    removed, cut into ¼-
    inch cubes
⅓ cup crumbled Roquefort
    or other blue cheese
2 tablespoons imported Dijon mustard
3 tablespoons red wine vinegar or balsamic vinegar
8 cups young dandelion greens or arugula, washed,
    trimmed, and spun dry
½ cup minced fresh chives
2 hard-cooked eggs, shredded (use a hand grater) or
    finely chopped
1 cup homemade garlic croutons (recipe follows)
Sea or coarse salt and freshly ground black pepper
    to taste

1. Preheat the oven to 350°F.

2. Cook the bacon in a heavy skillet over medium heat until crisp. With a slotted spoon, transfer the cooked bacon to a plate lined with paper towels and drain. Pour off all but ⅓ cup bacon fat from the skillet.

3. In a small bowl, mash together the Roquefort, mustard, and vinegar until smooth. Blend this mixture into the bacon fat in the skillet to make a homogenous dressing.

4. In a large stainless-steel (or other ovenproof) bowl, mix together the greens, chives, shredded hard-cooked eggs, reserved bacon, and garlic croutons. Place the bowl in the oven to begin to wilt the greens slightly, about 3 minutes.

5. While the greens are wilting, heat the dressing in the skillet over medium-high heat until sizzling hot. Immediately pour the hot dressing over the warm greens (remembering to use pot holders because the salad bowl will be very hot) and toss well. Season the salad with sea salt and freshly ground pepper and serve at once.

MAKES 4 SERVINGS

67

GARLIC CROUTONS

There's no excuse for buying mediocre packaged croutons when making your own is so simple and the results are so much more delicious.

1½ tablespoons olive oil
1½ tablespoons unsalted butter
2 cups day-old French bread cubes (½-inch cubes)
1 clove garlic, minced
Sea or coarse salt and freshly ground black pepper
    to taste

1. Heat the oil and butter together in a medium-size skillet over medium heat. Add the bread cubes and toss to coat evenly with the oil and butter. Reduce the heat to low and sauté the bread, stirring frequently, until toasted light golden brown, 15 to 20 minutes.

2. Stir in the garlic and continue to sauté 4 to 5 minutes longer to infuse the croutons with the garlic flavor. Remove from heat, season with salt and pepper, and let cool to room temperature. If not using within a few hours, store the croutons in an airtight container or plastic bag for up to 4 days.

MAKES 2 CUPS

Asparagus with Aigrelette Sauce

French cuisine honors the arrival and duration of asparagus season better than any other I know. The original *aigrelette* sauce is the invention of southern Burgundy's Georges Blanc—the youngest chef ever to receive a three-star rating from the *Guide Michelin,* and his sauce does indeed do poetic justice to the season's best asparagus. Georges Blanc uses his *aigrelette* to sauce salmon slices fired for a mere minute in a 550°F oven; I encourage home cooks to explore the versatility of my interpretation of this rich vinaigrette by pairing it with simply poached fish and other vegetables.

1 large egg yolk (optional; see recipe introduction,
     page 61)
1 tablespoon imported Dijon mustard
1½ tablespoons fresh lemon juice
⅓ cup peanut oil
¼ cup vegetable oil
¼ cup fruity olive oil
2 tablespoons white Burgundy wine
1 tablespoon white wine vinegar
2 tablespoons chicken broth
½ cup assorted minced fresh herbs (any combination of
     parsley, chives, tarragon, chervil, dill, cilantro, and/or
     basil works well)
Sea or coarse salt and freshly ground black pepper
     to taste
2 pounds medium asparagus, trimmed and bottom
     portion of stalks peeled

69

1. In a medium-size bowl, whisk together the egg yolk, mustard, and lemon juice. Slowly whisk in the peanut, vegetable, and olive oils to form a thickened emulsion. Whisk in the wine, vinegar, and broth. Season with the fresh herbs and salt and pepper. Refrigerate the sauce if not using within the hour, but let it return to room temperature before using.

2. Place the asparagus spears in a wide saucepan and add water just to cover. Bring the water to a boil and cook the asparagus, uncovered, until crisp-tender, 3 to 4 minutes. Drain well and immediately sauce with enough *aigrelette* to coat the spears lightly and evenly. (Save the remaining sauce for another time. It will keep, covered and refrigerated, for 3 to 4 days with the yolk added and for 1 week without it.) Serve hot, warm, or at room temperature.

MAKES 6 TO 8 SERVINGS

French Lentil Salad

It's one thing to talk about that distinctly French notion of *terroir* when explaining why the country's vineyards produce wines of such worldly renown, but it is quite another to apply the same notion as an explanation of why humble green lentils from Le Puy, in the Massif Central, taste so much better than American-grown ones. Yet, they do! They do! And *lentilles du Puy* seem currently to be not only the darlings of all France but also of many specialty food shops, which is where they may be purchased stateside in order to make this delicious salad.

Most French lentil salads are simple affairs dotted with a few minced vegetables and bathed in a tangy vinaigrette. In thinking about how much I would enjoy such a salad on a day's biking and picnic excursion to the spectacular fifteenth-century Flemish-tiled Château de la Rochepot, southwest of Beaune, I created my version of a lentil salad fortified with strips of the region's hard sausage, for which I tend to have an incredible weakness.

2 cups French lentils (lentilles du Puy)
2 cups chicken stock, preferably homemade
2 cups water
1 cup dry white wine
2 bay leaves
2 carrots, peeled and cut into ¼-inch dice
1 small red onion, minced
8 ounces hard sausage, such as Abruzze or
    hard salami, cut into 2-inch-long
    julienne sticks

VINAIGRETTE
2 cloves garlic, minced
2 tablespoons imported Dijon mustard
3 tablespoons red wine vinegar
⅔ cup olive oil
1 tablespoon minced fresh thyme leaves, or 1 teaspoon
    dried thyme
1 cup minced fresh parsley
Sea or coarse salt and freshly ground black
    pepper to taste

71

1. Place the lentils in a medium-size saucepan and cover with the chicken stock, water, and white wine. Add the bay leaves. Bring to a boil over medium-high heat and simmer for 20 minutes. Add the carrots and onion to the saucepan and continue cooking until the lentils are tender, 10 to 15 minutes more.

2. Drain the lentil mixture, but be sure to leave just a couple of tablespoons of the cooking liquid to keep the lentils moist. Discard the bay leaves and toss the warm lentil mixture with the sausage in a large mixing bowl.

3. To make the vinaigrette, whisk together the garlic, mustard,

and red wine vinegar. Slowly whisk in the olive oil. Pour the vinai-grette over the lentil mixture while it is still warm, stirring gently. Mix in the thyme and the parsley. Season the salad to taste with salt and pepper. The salad may be served slightly warm or at room temperature.

MAKES 6 SERVINGS

TOASTING NUTS

I n Burgundy, when there's talk of toasting, it is usu-ally either in reference to charring oak barrels in which wine is aged to impart subtle smoky flavors or the clinking of cyclists' glasses in celebration of a day well biked.

In the text of this book, however, toasting is confined to nuts. I frequently toast the nuts used in my recipes to make their flavor even nuttier. If it is only a handful of nuts that needs to be toasted, use the toaster oven set at 350°F. The nuts should be checked after 5 minutes and then monitored closely for the next couple of min-utes until they turn a light golden brown and are fragrant. The unwatched nut almost always burns, and most, in the toaster oven, take between 5 and 8 minutes to become perfectly toasted. For larger amounts of nuts, I use my regular oven, also set to 350°F. I spread the nuts in a single lay-er in a baking pan and begin monitoring them closely after about 3 minutes. Nuts toasted in the oven will take between 8 and 10 minutes to brown lightly.

Jambon Persillé
à Ma Façon

⌒

Even though I feel gloriously at one with Burgundy's wine, I am convinced that I was never a Burgundian in a past life, as my palate demonstrates a serious lack of enthusiasm for many of the area's most prized regional recipes. *Jambon persillé*—a terrine consisting of chunks of ham suspended in a chardonnay-flavored aspic laden with parsley, garlic, and shallots—is a perfect example of what I'm talking about, for it is frequently the butt of many a cyclist's joke as we travel through the region that reveres it. While a thick slice of this mélange may well be the perfect appetizer to savor with a fine glass of Chablis, Puligny-Montrachet, or Meursault, I tend not to like anything served to me in slab form, let alone suspended in aspic. No wonder Burgundy-born Colette said, "Burgundy is like a pig: Some parts are more memorable than others, but every bit is edible."

Never one, however, to pass up an occasion for enjoying a fine glass of white Burgundy with anything, I set out to devise my own personally more palatable rendition of the region's parsleyed ham. Aspic instantly eliminated, I found myself faced with ingredients that would lend themselves quite nicely to a salad, particularly with a little additional enhancement from some non-traditional Gruyère cheese and a hearty sprinkling of coarsely chopped pistachio nuts.

The ham used in this recipe should be a mild baked or boiled one from a delicatessen—or even better, look for the Madrange Company's Le Jambon Français, imported from France and increas-

73

ingly available in the United States. This *jambon persillé* done "my way" still works well as a first course and should be mounded onto a bed of buttery green lettuce leaves. The salad is also a natural for cyclists to pack when bound for a wine-country picnic.

> 1 pound thinly sliced baked or boiled mild ham
> ½ pound thinly sliced French or Swiss Gruyère or
>   other Swiss cheese
> 2 shallots, minced
> 2 cloves garlic, minced
> 1½ cups minced fresh parsley
> ½ cup shelled pistachio nuts, lightly toasted (see box,
>   page 72) and coarsely chopped
> 8 cornichons (small French pickles), drained and
>   minced
> 2 tablespoons imported Dijon mustard
> ½ cup white Burgundy wine or other chardonnay
> ½ cup peanut oil or other mild vegetable oil
> Sea or coarse salt and freshly ground black pepper
>   to taste

1. Cut both the ham and cheese into ½-inch squares and toss together in a large mixing bowl. Stir in the shallots, garlic, parsley, pistachios, and cornichons.

2. Whisk together the mustard and wine in a small bowl. Slowly whisk in the oil. Pour the dressing over the salad, tossing gently to combine. Season the salad to taste with salt and pepper and serve at once or chill until serving time. The salad is best when served slightly chilled or at room temperature; it will keep for up to 3 days in the refrigerator.

MAKES 6 SERVINGS

Warm Potato and Sausage Salad Lyonnaise

This is the sort of hearty dish that always tickles my salad-and-sausage-loving fancy at bistro-style restaurants throughout Burgundy and in Lyons.

The French always seem to peel their potatoes after, rather than before, boiling. While peeling steaming-hot potatoes can be a bit tough on the hands, I have found there to be more wisdom than masochism to the method. Boiling potatoes in the jacket seems to maximize the naturally earthy flavor of the tubers.

Dressing the potatoes while hot adds to the delightful appeal of this salad because the flavors of the wine, mustard, and vinegar are readily absorbed into the potato chunks. While a *salade lyonnaise* is always served hot or warm in bistros, I find it equally tasty at room temperature and therefore recommend it as perfect picnic fare to fuel a day of vigorous Hautes-Côtes (hilly!!!) biking.

75

3 pounds boiling potatoes
1½ pounds garlicky sausage, such as kielbasa or French
    saucisson à l'ail
3 tablespoons white wine vinegar
1½ tablespoons imported Dijon mustard
½ cup dry white Burgundy wine or other chardonnay
½ cup olive oil or vegetable oil
Sea or coarse salt and freshly ground black pepper to taste
1 bunch scallions, trimmed and thinly sliced on the diagonal
½ cup minced fresh parsley

1. Place the potatoes in a large pot and cover amply with cold water. Bring to a boil and simmer, uncovered, until just tender but not mushy, 25 to 30 minutes. Drain in a colander.

2. While the potatoes are cooking, place the sausage in a small saucepan and cover with cold water. Bring to a boil and then simmer, uncovered, for 15 minutes and drain.

3. Whisk together the vinegar, mustard, wine, and oil in a small bowl.

4. Peel the hot potatoes, perhaps using a clean dish towel to help protect your fingers from the heat, and then slice them ½ inch thick and place in a large mixing bowl. Immediately pour the dressing over the warm potatoes, tossing well to coat all over.

5. Slice the sausage on the diagonal into ½-inch-thick slices and add to the potatoes, tossing well again. Season the salad to taste with salt and pepper. Mix in the scallions and parsley and serve the salad warm or at room temperature.

76

MAKES 6 TO 8 SERVINGS

Burgundy Onions

W hile I can guiltlessly forgo including in this collection heavy and traditional recipes for *boeuf bourguignonne* and *coq au vin,* I have become convinced that the peeling of little onions—and lots of them—is one of those unpleasant tasks that must be accepted by anyone aspiring to Burgundian culinary triumph.

The good news is that this recipe is sort of a beginner's warm-up, since the onions being peeled are 1-inch boiling onions, rather than the smaller (and peskier) pearl onions. Once the nasty peeling has been accomplished, the onions are browned in butter, simmered in a sea of red wine, and then reduced with a little sugar so that they emerge coated with a sweet and glistening Burgundy glaze. All said and done, these onions are delicious and make a fine accompaniment to most meat dishes.

2 pounds boiling onions (1½ to 2 inches
  in diameter)
2 tablespoons unsalted butter
1½ cups red Burgundy table wine
1 tablespoon sugar
Freshly ground black pepper to taste

77

1. Trim the hairy stems from the ends of the onions. Bring a large pot of water to a boil and blanch the onions for 1 minute. Drain the onions, and when they are cool enough to handle, gently slip off and discard the skins.

2. Melt the butter over medium heat in a large skillet. Add the onions and shake the pan frequently to lightly brown them all over, 8 to 10 minutes. Pour the wine into the skillet, cover, and reduce the heat to medium-low. Simmer the onions in the wine until they are tender, about 30 minutes.

3. Sprinkle the sugar evenly over the onions and bring the liquid in the pan to a boil. Cook until the liquid is reduced to a syrupy glaze, 5 to 7 minutes. Season the onions with pepper and serve hot.

MAKES 6 TO 8 SERVINGS

French Carrots

I learned this method of cooking intensely flavored carrots not in France but at home reading fellow author Richard Grausman's cookbook *At Home with the French Classics*. This recipe is derived from an old, venerable dish, known in the native tongue as *carottes Vichy,* in which carrots were cooked—originally for health reasons—in revitalizing Vichy mineral water until it had completely evaporated.

Richard's recipe goes one bold step further by eliminating the cooking water altogether in order to let the carrots steep gently in their own inherent moisture, resulting in a heightened natural sweetness that he says always garners raves from his cooking students. The recipe gets equal raves from me, since it is capable of making any old carrots taste as sensational as those sprung from fertile Burgundy soil and adds the perfect vegetable accent to many of the region's meaty main courses.

During the summer months, I am fond of finishing my "waterless" carrots with a generous sprinkling of fresh herbs—dill, chives, chervil, or tarragon. In colder months, finely chopped crystallized ginger or a sprinkling of anise or caraway seeds makes for a perky addition.

2 tablespoons unsalted butter

1½ pounds baby carrots, trimmed, peeled, and sliced
    lengthwise in half

3 tablespoons minced fresh dill, chives, chervil,
    or tarragon

Sea or coarse salt and freshly ground black pepper to taste

1. Melt the butter in a medium-size skillet with 2- to 3-inch sides over medium-low heat. Add the carrots and cover the pan with a tight-fitting lid. Cook the carrots over medium-low heat, shaking the pan from time to time; the carrots should be steaming slowly in their own moisture but not browning. Cook until the carrots are crisp-tender, about 15 to 20 minutes. If there is any excess moisture from the carrots remaining in the bottom of the pan, remove the lid and increase the heat until all of the liquid has evaporated.

2. Add the herb of your choice to the carrots and toss to coat evenly. Season to taste with salt and pepper. Serve at once as an accompaniment to meat and poultry dishes.

MAKES 6 SERVINGS

Summer Squash with White Wine and Cracked Coriander Seeds

This recipe is adapted from the 1992 *L'Almanach Bourguignon,* a charmingly illustrated regional almanac sold in selected newspaper and bookstores throughout Burgundy. I like the recipe because it is often difficult to find an aromatic yet light vegetable accompaniment to the riches of Burgundy cuisine. In the original version the squash is served well chilled, but I'm happier serving it warm or at room temperature.

3 tablespoons olive oil

1 medium onion, minced

2 small, young summer (yellow) squash (about ⅔ pound),
    sliced into ¼-inch-thick rounds

2 small, young zucchini (about ⅔ pound), sliced
    into ¼-inch-thick rounds

1 cup white Burgundy table wine or other
    chardonnay

1½ teaspoons whole coriander seeds, coarsely
    ground (use a mortar and pestle or
    spice grinder)

Sea or coarse salt and freshly ground black
    pepper to taste

Pinch of sugar

2 tablespoons fresh lemon juice

2 cloves garlic, minced

⅓ cup minced fresh chervil or parsley

1. Heat the olive oil in a large skillet over medium heat. Add the onion and sauté until it begins to brown, 7 to 8 minutes. Add the summer squash and zucchini, tossing to coat with the oil and onions. Pour in the wine and season with the coriander seeds, salt, pepper, and sugar. Cover the pan and simmer over medium-low heat until the squash is tender and about half the wine has evaporated, about 20 minutes.

2. Remove the squash mixture from the heat and toss gently with the lemon juice, garlic, and chervil. Cover the pan and set aside until ready to serve. Serve warm or at room temperature.

MAKES 4 TO 6 SERVINGS

Grilled Mushrooms with Escargot's Butter

∽

It could well be said that savoring the Burgundy countryside by bicycle gives one an *escargot's-*eye view of an area where the *escargot* is indeed celebrated. Cycling at near a snail's pace allows for time to appreciate the spectacular way in which the sunlight dances off the Flemish roof tiles in the sleepy village of Corton-Charlemagne, time to smell the same subtle nuances of barnyard and wild berry patch that will later emanate from the evening's bottle of red wine, and time to work up the sort of appetite that says, "Yes, I can enjoy the same rich butter that bathes Burgundy's *escargots* on my mushrooms, too."

Mushrooms seem to have as much of an affinity for this garlicky butter as the snails for which it was originally designed, but in addition to being served as an appetizer, the mushrooms also make a fine accompaniment to succulent cuts of beef and lamb. Common white mushrooms are suitable in the recipe, but don't hesitate to use cremini, shiitake, portobello, or porcini caps if you happen to spy them in the market.

81

8 tablespoons (1 stick) unsalted butter
⅓ cup white Burgundy table wine or other chardonnay
3 large cloves garlic, minced
2 tablespoons fresh thyme leaves or 1½ teaspoons dried thyme
½ cup minced fresh parsley
Sea or coarse salt and freshly ground black pepper to taste
2½ pounds firm fresh mushrooms (see above for recommended varieties), stems removed

1. Prepare an outdoor fire for grilling or preheat the broiler.

2. Melt the butter in a small saucepan over medium-low heat. Stir in the wine, garlic, thyme, and parsley. Season with salt and pepper. Place the mushroom caps in a large mixing bowl and pour the butter over them, tossing the mushrooms well to coat evenly.

3. Arrange the mushroom caps, all facing up or down, over the bottom half of a hinged, metal grill basket or in a large broiler pan. Set the mushrooms 5 inches away from the heat and grill or broil until lightly colored on one side, 6 to 7 minutes. Turn over the basket or the mushrooms and continue cooking until the other sides are also lightly colored, another 6 to 7 minutes. Serve the mushrooms hot. A little bit of bread is always welcome for sopping up any extra butter and juices.

MAKES 6 SERVINGS

Delicious White Beans in a Light Wine and Cream Sauce

Large white shell beans, called *haricots blancs* in French, cooked to crisp-tender perfection and then napped with an aromatic cream- or broth-based sauce are all the rage these days in Burgundy restaurants. Now, stateside, there's no reason for me mere-

ly to dream of the warm white bean and tongue salad served at Le Gourmandin in Beaune or the fabulous braised beans that are paired with rosy slices of rosemary-infused duck breast at Restaurant Lea in Montrevel-en-Bresse, when I can easily make my own. While these beans are a tasty accompaniment to many of the main courses in this book, I must confess to finding them quite tasty served just by themselves as home-alone comfort food.

1 pound dried large white lima or kidney beans,
    soaked in water to cover overnight
3 whole cloves
1 medium onion, peeled
1 large carrot, scrubbed and broken into thirds
1 ham hock
2 tablespoons unsalted butter
1 tablespoon olive or vegetable oil
3 shallots, minced
4 cloves garlic, minced
2 teaspoons dried tarragon
1 teaspoon dried thyme
¾ cup dry white Burgundy wine or other chardonnay
¾ cup heavy (or whipping) cream
Sea or coarse salt and freshly ground black pepper to taste

1. Drain and rinse the soaked beans. Place them in a large pot and cover amply with fresh water. Stick the whole cloves into the onion and add it to the pot along with the carrot pieces and ham hock. Bring to a boil and simmer, uncovered, until the beans are crisp-tender, 40 to 45 minutes. Drain, reserving 1 cup of the cooking liquid. Discard the onion and carrot and, if feeling industrious, pick off any meat from the ham hock and add it to the beans.

2. Heat the butter and oil together in a large skillet over medium heat. Add the shallots, garlic, tarragon, and thyme and sauté for 5 minutes. Pour in the wine and the cup of reserved cooking liquid from the beans and let the mixture cook over high heat until reduced by half, 8 to 10 minutes. Add the cream to the skillet and let the mixture continue to boil for a few minutes until slightly thickened. Reduce heat to low, stir in the drained beans, and simmer until the beans are heated through. Season to taste with sea salt and pepper and serve at once.

MAKES 8 SERVINGS

Montrachet Mashed Potatoes

When it comes to cooking in a Burgundy mode, I've been known to do some pretty outrageous things—like pour a bottle of Meursault with abandon into an *escargot* bisque. But let me immediately reassure all who live for the best white Burgundy wines by clarifying that the Montrachet in this recipe title refers, not to the *Grand Cru* wine of all *Grands Crus,* but to the chalky white goat cheese of the same name that is made in neighboring Burgundy villages. This is not to say, however, that an exorbitantly expensive bottle of Le Montrachet or Bâtard-Montrachet might not make a very fine accompaniment indeed to these humble yet *haute* mashed potatoes.

Garlic mashed potatoes seem to have become the darling of

American bistro cooking, but I find I have come to prefer the creamy tang of melted goat cheese to the bite of puréed garlic when pairing potatoes with rich Burgundian beef, chicken, or pork dishes. A knoll of Montrachet Mashed Potatoes with a Dijon Deviled Chicken half or rosy slice of Salt-Crusted Beef Tenderloin accompanied by, say, a dusty old bottle of Chambolle-Musigny and a teetotaling but otherwise engaging friend is my idea of a heavenly French meal!

3 pounds boiling potatoes, peeled and cut into 2½-inch chunks

3 tablespoons unsalted butter, at room temperature

8 ounces imported or domestic Montrachet-style goat cheese, either plain or with herbs, at room temperature

½ cup white Burgundy wine or other chardonnay

⅓ cup half-and-half

Sea or coarse salt and freshly ground white pepper to taste

85
....

1. Place the potatoes in a large pot, cover with cold water, and bring them to a boil over medium-high heat. Simmer the potatoes, uncovered, until very tender, 25 to 30 minutes.

2. Drain the potatoes very well and purée them while still piping hot by passing them through a ricer or food mill. Using an electric hand mixer, beat in the butter and goat cheese until smooth. Thin the potatoes by beating in the wine and half-and-half. Season to taste with salt and white pepper. Serve at once or reheat later by zapping the potatoes in a microwave at high power for a few minutes, or until heated through.

MAKES 6 TO 8 SERVINGS

WHEN IN DIJON

Throughout the centuries, people of diverse origins have met in Dijon as they have traveled from north to south or east to west, and it is in this historic city, the regional capital of Burgundy, that my cyclists convene before heading south for a week of riding through the tidy patchwork of verdant vineyards and farms. Most will have arrived the day before the designated rendezvous to allow time to nose around the cobblestoned streets of Old Dijon and take in the timber-framed medieval houses of rue Verrerie or hear the famous Jacquemart family figures ringing the clock bells atop the Gothic and gargoyled Notre Dame church. I personally like to squeeze in a visit to the Musée des Beaux Arts, for I enjoy the museum's mix of period-furnished rooms with its impressive and eclectic array of Flemish, Swiss, German, Italian, Dutch, and Burgundian paintings. Not to be missed is the ground-floor ducal kitchen, where feasts of unimaginable magnitude were once prepared for the powerful Valois dukes of Burgundy. Six huge fireplaces for roasting whole venison and oxen line the expansive stone room, and the sight always whets my appetite for the grandeur of the meals I know will soon follow your days of biking.

Potato Gratin Dijonnaise

O ne of the best shops in Dijon is the old-fashioned Moutarde Grey Poupon store, where the city's namesake famous mustard may be purchased along with colorful, hand-painted porcelain mustard pots. I almost always run into members from our group here, carrying on one last mustard-buying frenzy, before they must board the bus that will carry them from Dijon to their bikes. Such memories conspire to make me crave the fiery kick of real Dijon mustard when it comes to making a French-style potato gratin to accompany one experimental red-wine-soused *boeuf* recipe or another. Suddenly, I think, why make a traditional and creamy old *Dauphinoise* when I can have a sunny yellow and pungent gratin *Dijonnaise*? *Voilà*—now I'm happiest having my potatoes and mustard, too!

87

3 pounds potatoes (about 6 large ones)
2 tablespoons unsalted butter
1 large yellow onion, thinly sliced
Sea or coarse salt and freshly ground black pepper
    to taste
2 tablespoons chopped fresh chervil, or 2 teaspoons
    dried
½ cup chopped fresh parsley
2 cups crème fraîche
3 heaping tablespoons imported Dijon mustard
¼ cup fresh lemon juice
4 ounces freshly grated Gruyère or Emmenthaler cheese

1. Place the potatoes in a large pot and cover with water. Bring to a boil over medium-high heat and cook until just barely tender when pierced in the center with a small knife. Drain and let stand until cool enough to handle. Remove the skins. Slice the potatoes into ⅓-inch-thick rounds.

2. While the potatoes are cooking and cooling, melt the butter in a small skillet over medium heat. Add the onion and sauté, stirring frequently, until light golden brown, about 15 minutes. Remove from the heat.

3. Preheat the oven to 400°F. Butter a shallow 12-inch-wide gratin dish and set aside.

4. Gently combine the sliced potatoes and sautéed onion in a large mixing bowl. Season with the salt, pepper, chervil, and parsley.

5. In a small mixing bowl, whisk together the crème fraîche, mustard, and lemon juice until smooth. Gently but thoroughly combine this mixture with the potato-onion mixture. Turn all into the prepared gratin dish and arrange evenly. Sprinkle the grated cheese over the top of the potatoes.

6. Bake the gratin in the oven until bubbly and lightly browned on top, about 30 minutes. Let cool a few minutes and serve.

MAKES 8 TO 10 SERVINGS

Note: Leftovers, if any, seem to taste even better reheated the following day.

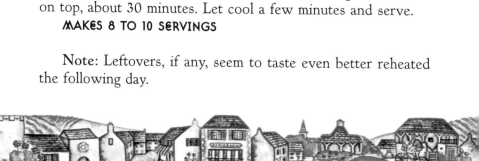

Simply
Steamed New Potatoes

I almost never encounter steamed potatoes in America, yet whenever I'm served *pommes de terre vapeur* in Burgundian bistros, I am amazed by how something so basic can taste so marvelous. Steaming seems to concentrate and heighten the natural earthiness of the potatoes, and when care is taken to peel a center stripe around each little pink-skinned potato, they end up looking picture perfect on the plate.

2 pounds new or small red potatoes
3 tablespoons unsalted butter, melted
⅓ cup minced fresh parsley
Sea or coarse salt and freshly ground black pepper to taste

89

1. Peel away a 1-inch-wide strip of skin around the center of each potato.

2. Pour water into a medium-size saucepan to come about 1½ inches up the sides and bring to a boil. Lower the heat to a simmer and insert a metal basket steamer into the pot, making sure that the water does not rise above the base of the steamer (pour out the extra water if it does). Add the potatoes and cover and steam until they feel tender but not mushy when pierced with a toothpick, 20 to 30 minutes.

3. Remove the potatoes from the steamer and place in a serving bowl. Toss with the melted butter and parsley and season with salt and pepper. Serve at once.

MAKES 6 SERVINGS

Pumpkin and Potato Gratin

I n Burgundy, there is a widely prevalent theory that grapevines must struggle to produce fine wine. Likewise, there is nothing like a nippy and drizzly day spent on a bicycle during autumn in the Côte d'Or to make Burgundy's hearty fare taste all the more welcome. Truth be told, the precious harvest is not the only thing affected by lack of sunshine! While braking/breaking for the occasional tasting descent into a local wine cellar might seem like the perfect antidote to biking in the rain, cellars by nature must be dark, damp, and dank places. All of a sudden, that rotund *pot-iron,* or French pumpkin, last spied cut into huge crescent wedges on market day, is beginning to seem awfully enticing.

90

Indeed, pumpkin is a staple of Burgundian cooking, and this sunny colored gratin is guaranteed to warm dampened cyclists and spirits.

4 cups peeled, seeded, and cubed fresh pumpkin or
   butternut squash
4 large potatoes, peeled and cubed
1 large red onion, unpeeled, quartered
8 slices bacon
4 tablespoons (½ stick) unsalted butter, at room temperature
3 large eggs, at room temperature
1¼ cups shredded Gruyère cheese
½ teaspoon freshly grated nutmeg
Sea or coarse salt and freshly ground black pepper to taste
1 cup fresh bread crumbs

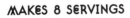
1. Combine the pumpkin, potatoes, and onion in a large pot, cover amply with water, and boil until tender, 25 to 30 minutes.

2. Preheat the oven to 400°F.

3. While the vegetables are cooking, sauté the bacon in a skillet until it is just beginning to crisp. Drain the bacon on paper towels, reserving 2 tablespoons of the fat. Brush the fat over the bottom of a shallow, 2-quart gratin dish. Set aside.

4. Drain the boiled vegetables well in a colander. Discard the skin from the onion and set the onion quarters aside. Using either an electric hand mixer or a vegetable masher, mash the potatoes and pumpkin together in a large mixing bowl until well combined. Mash in 3 tablespoons of the butter until it is melted, and then beat in the eggs and 1 cup of the Gruyère cheese. Season all with nutmeg and salt and pepper to taste.

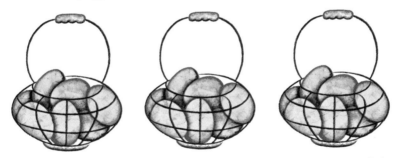

.91
.··.

5. Layer the reserved onion segments over the bottom of the gratin dish. Spread the pumpkin-potato mixture evenly over the onions. Blend the remaining 1 tablespoon butter with the bread crumbs and then sprinkle them evenly over the top of the gratin. Crumble the bacon and dot the crumbs with it plus the remaining ¼ cup shredded Gruyère.

6. Bake the gratin until the top has a light golden-brown crust, 25 to 30 minutes. Serve hot as a rich side dish.

MAKES 8 SERVINGS

UNCOMPLICATED HUNGER

THERE IN DIJON, the cauliflowers were small and very succulent, grown in that ancient soil. I separated the flowerets and dropped them into boiling water for just a few minutes. Then I drained them and put them in a wide shallow casserole, and covered them with heavy cream and a thick sprinkling of freshly grated Gruyère, the nice rubbery kind that didn't come from Switzerland at all, but from the Jura. It was called râpé in the market, and was grated while you watched, in a soft cloudy pile, onto your piece of paper.

I put some fresh pepper over the top, and in a way I can't remember how the little tin oven heated the whole thing and melted the cheese and browned it. As soon as that happened we ate it.

The cream and cheese had come together into a perfect sauce, and the little flowers were tender and fresh. We cleaned our plates with bits of crisp bread crust and drank the wine, and Al and Lawrence planned to write books about Aristotle and Robinson Jeffers and probably themselves, and I planned a few things, too.

As I say, once back in California, after so many of those casseroles, I found I could never make one. The vegetable was watery, and there was no cream thick enough or unpasteurized and fresh. The cheese was dry and oily, not soft and light. I had to make a sauce with flour in it. I could concoct a good dish, still . . . but it was never so innocent, so simple . . . and then where was the crisp bread, where the honest wine? And where were our young uncomplicated hungers, too?

—M.F.K. FISHER
LONG AGO IN FRANCE

Cauliflower Gratinée in Honor of M.F.K. Fisher

I t's no secret that books often make good, if not better, traveling companions than human beings. And it just wouldn't be right not to honor here the late M.F.K. Fisher's writing about her early matrimonial days in Burgundy in the late 1920s and early '30s, currently published under the title *Long Ago in France—The Years in Dijon.* For as long as I can remember, passages from these recollections have formed a kaleidoscopic frame of reference for me in my own travels in Burgundy.

After Fisher and her husband had spent two years living as boarders in Dijon, they got their own little apartment in a "low quarter" of town, where the author discovered that cooking: "was only a little less complicated than performing an appendectomy on a life raft, but after I got used to hauling water and putting together three courses on a table the size of a bandanna, and lighting the portable stove without blowing myself clear into the living room instead of only halfway, it was fun."

A favorite Fisher meal revolved around a simple casserole of cauliflower, cream, and cheese, which she sadly discovered could never be duplicated back home in California since American cauliflowers were more watery and the cream less thick than French counterparts. After reading about Fisher's difficulties transplanting this dish, it became my personal challenge to make the recipe succeed on Yankee soil. The first four tries failed, as the cauliflower and cream continued against all hope and reason to separate while in the oven. I tried the recipe in Burgundy under Fisheresque circumstances, lighting a little stove that nearly blew me into surrounding Côte de Beaune vineyards, and . . . it worked!

Just when I was ready to scratch all homefront efforts, an Italian friend suggested that I make the gratinée with mascarpone cheese instead of crème fraîche to compensate for the strange wateriness of our domestic cauliflower. Well, the fifth attempt proved to be the charm, and I do think that M.F.K. Fisher herself would have approved of my American version since I succeeded in making it taste like the French one without resorting to a thickening roux.

1 medium head cauliflower
1 cup mascarpone cheese
Sea or coarse salt and freshly ground white pepper to taste
Pinch of freshly grated nutmeg
Pinch of cayenne pepper
4 ounces Gruyère cheese

1. Preheat the oven to 375°F. Butter a shallow, 1½-quart round or oval gratin dish.

2. Trim the cauliflower and break it into bite-size florets. Steam the cauliflower over boiling water until cooked halfway through, 3 to 5 minutes; remove from the heat immediately. Season the mascarpone with the salt, white pepper, nutmeg, and cayenne. Add the cauliflower and mix it gently but thoroughly into the mascarpone. Transfer the mixture to the prepared baking dish.

3. Grate the Gruyère as finely as possible, using either a round Mouli grater or the small holes of a hand-held grater. Sprinkle the cheese evenly over the top of the cauliflower. Bake until bubbling and golden brown on top, 40 to 45 minutes. Serve at once with a chewy *baguette* and a chilled bottle of white Burgundy to one or two cherished but unpretentious friends.

MAKES 2 TO 3 SERVINGS FOR A SIMPLE BUT MEMORABLE MEAL

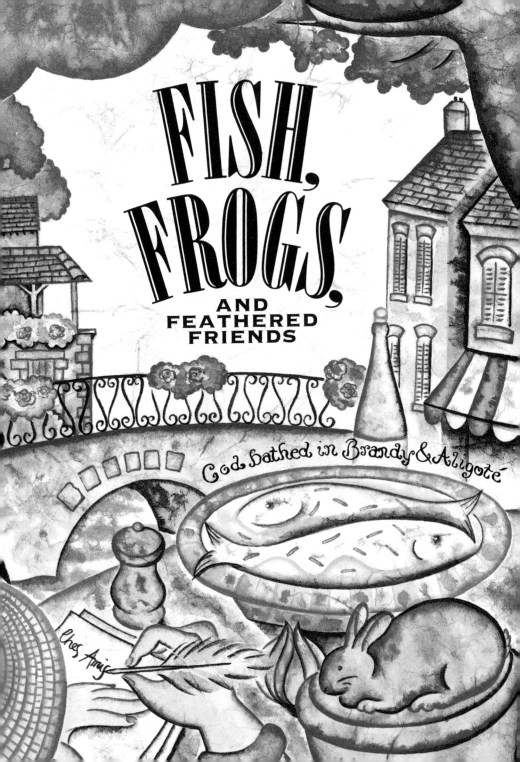

FISH, FROGS, AND FEATHERED FRIENDS

Cod bathed in Brandy & Aligoté

Burgundy's freshwater rivers, streams, and lakes teem with delicate fish and jump with that quintessential French delight: frogs. Chicken from the lush Bresse countryside is honored as the Rolls-Royce of poultry, and the Burgundy duck is mighty delectable, too. Where feathers fly, fur can't be far behind, and there's nothing better or more Burgundian than tender young rabbit spiked with Dijon mustard.

96

Crisped Salmon with Mustard Mousse

I first dined at Beaune's salmon-hued Restaurant le Central in the afternoon on a blustery March day. It was also that time of year when I was edging toward another one of those awful thirtysomething birthdays and therefore feeling vulnerably Piscean. My tender and morose sensibilities were soon transformed by attentive service and a *dégustation* menu of sheer fish bliss,

wherein everything was pink and cooked to perfection. I particularly marveled over my main-course salmon: The fillet was delectably crusted on top, having been dusted with aromatic cracked coriander seeds and roasted in a very hot oven. Poetic interpretations of the sea further enhanced my plate in the form of blanched green seaweed tendrils and a most unusual mustard mousse that brought to mind the froth of a curling ocean wave and to palate an exciting and novel mustard taste sensation.

Over the course of the next year, I searched in vain through French cookbooks for a mustard mousse recipe that I thought might be similar and dreamt of my luncheon before having the good fortune of returning to Restaurant le Central. Sadly, the salmon wasn't on the day's menu, but chef Jean Garcin was graciously willing to engage in a rewarding chat and share his inventive mustard mousse recipe with me.

97

MUSTARD MOUSSE
2 large shallots, minced
¼ cup white wine vinegar
¼ cup dry white wine
3 tablespoons imported coarse-grained Dijon mustard
3 large egg whites
Sea or coarse salt and freshly ground black pepper to taste
1 to 2 teaspoons imported smooth Dijon mustard

SALMON
6 salmon fillets (6 to 8 ounces each)
3 tablespoons unsalted butter, melted
½ cup dry white wine
1½ teaspoons coarsely cracked coriander seeds
Sea or coarse salt and freshly ground black pepper
    to taste

1. Preheat the oven to 425°F.

2. To make the mustard mousse, place the shallots, vinegar, and wine in a small skillet and bring to a boil over medium-high heat. Continue cooking until the liquid has almost entirely evaporated, 6 to 8 minutes. Remove the skillet from the heat and swirl in the coarse mustard.

3. In a medium-size bowl, beat the egg whites until they hold soft peaks. Gently but thoroughly fold in the hot mustard and shallot mixture. Season the mousse to taste with salt and pepper and enhance the mustard flavor by folding in 1 or 2 teaspoons of smooth Dijon mustard. Keep the mousse warm by placing the bowl over a pan of hot but not boiling water.

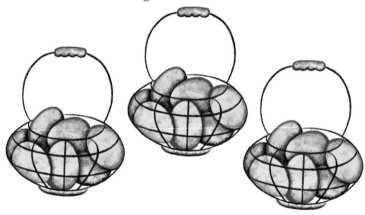

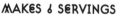

4. Arrange the salmon fillets in a roasting pan and drizzle them with the melted butter and wine. Sprinkle the cracked coriander seeds evenly over the top and then season with salt and pepper. Roast the salmon until lightly crisped on the top and just barely cooked through the center, about 10 minutes. Serve the fillets hot from the oven, drizzled with any pan juices and accompanied by a generous dollop of the mustard mousse.

MAKES 6 SERVINGS

Quintessential
Quenelles

ᡁ

O ne of the first things that attracted me to my business part-
ner, with whom I ran a restaurant on Nantucket for a tor-
tuous year and a half, was that he adored *quenelles.* Now, it is not
every day that you run into someone who is familiar with, let
alone has a passion for, these feathery fish dumplings that are a
specialty of *charcuteries* in Lyons and restaurants throughout Burgundy. In retrospect, it is unfortunate that our restaurant and
partnership could not have thrived on a shared love for *quenelles*
alone.

Like most traditional French dishes, *quenelles,* with all their
subtlety of flavor and velvetiness of texture, do not arrive at the
table without some diligent efforts on the part of the cook. In
France, *quenelles* are usually made from pike, or *brochet,* which is
puréed and then mixed with a *panade* or *choux* pastry, before being
shaped, poached, and napped with a variety of cream or tomato-
based sauces.

At home, I make my *quenelles* from flounder or sole and am
able to eliminate the step of making a separate *choux* pastry by
mixing my fish, eggs, and softened butter all together in a food
processor and then chilling the mixture for a good 12 hours or
overnight before making the dumplings. The one extra-labor-inten-
sive precaution I do employ is passing the *quenelle* mixture through
a sieve to ensure sublimely smooth and light dumplings. In America, I've noticed the tendency of chefs to pair *quenelles* with tomato sauce, but I think there is no more divine combination in the

99

world than the classic one of *quenelles* with a *sauce Nantua,* or Crayfish Cream (page 22). Another simple yet delicious alternative to *sauce Nantua* would be the saffron-and-curry-scented *velouté* recipe included here.

QUENELLES
1 pound flounder or sole fillets, skin and bones entirely removed
4 large eggs
1 cup heavy (or whipping) cream
2 teaspoons sea or coarse salt
Freshly ground white pepper to taste
¼ teaspoon cayenne pepper
¼ teaspoon ground nutmeg
4 tablespoons (½ stick) unsalted butter, at room temperature
Unbleached all-purpose flour, for shaping the quenelles
¾ cup dry white wine

VELOUTÉ
3 tablespoons unsalted butter
¼ cup unbleached all-purpose flour
½ teaspoon saffron threads
½ teaspoon curry powder
2 cups fish stock or bottled clam juice
½ cup heavy (or whipping) cream
Sea or coarse salt and freshly ground white pepper to taste

1. The day before you plan to poach the *quenelles,* cut the fish into 1-inch pieces and purée them in a food processor. With the machine running, add the eggs, one at a time, and keep processing until absolutely smooth. With the machine still running, add the heavy cream. Season the mixture with 1 teaspoon of the salt, the pepper, cayenne, and nutmeg. Cut the butter into small pieces, add them to the food processor, and continue processing until the butter is thoroughly incorporated. Pass the *quenelle* mixture through a fine-meshed sieve. Transfer it to a bowl, cover, and refrigerate for at least 12 hours.

2. To shape the *quenelle* mixture into dumplings, have ready a clean surface dusted lightly all over with the flour. Drop spoonfuls of the mixture the size of a small egg onto the surface and roll them with the palm of your hand into uniform oval shapes. Transfer the *quenelles* to a tray and repeat the process, adding more flour as needed to prevent sticking.

3. To poach the *quenelles,* pour water into a wide, shallow saucepan to a depth of 2 inches. Add the wine and the remaining 1 teaspoon salt. Bring to a simmer over medium heat. Drop 7 or 8 *quenelles* into the simmering liquid and poach until they float to the top and are just cooked through the centers, 6 to 8 minutes. Take care to maintain the poaching liquid at a simmer rather than full boil. Remove the cooked *quenelles* from the pan with a slotted spoon, draining well; set aside on a tray. Continue poaching the rest of the *quenelles* in the same manner. (The *quenelles* may be made ahead to this point and refrigerated for 1 or 2 days before the final baking.)

4. If making the *velouté* sauce, melt the butter in a medium-size saucepan over medium heat. Whisk in the flour until smooth and continue cooking, whisking constantly, for 2 minutes. (Do not let this roux brown.) Whisk in the saffron and curry powder. Slowly whisk in the fish stock and continue cooking and whisking until the sauce is smooth and thickened, 4 to 5 minutes. Whisk in the heavy cream and cook a minute or so more. Season the *velouté* to taste with salt and pepper. The sauce may be used at once, or refrigerated for up to 4 days and reheated for later use.

5. When ready to bake the *quenelles,* preheat the oven to 375°F.

6. The *quenelles* may be arranged either in a large gratin dish or individual dishes, allowing 3 to 4 *quenelles* per person. Nap the *quenelles* generously with either the warmed *velouté* sauce or a *sauce*

101
.....

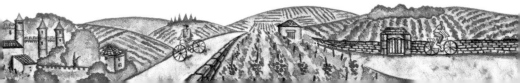

Nantua and bake until the sauce is bubbling and the tops of the *quenelles* are puffed and golden, 25 to 30 minutes. Serve at once.

MAKES 6 SERVINGS, OR 20 TO 22 QUENELLES

MARC DE BOURGOGNE

*M*arc is the potent and unforgettable result of wine-making thriftiness. After all of the juice has been extracted from grapes for the making of wine, the remaining mass of skins, seeds, and stems is distilled into a fiery, two-to-three-digit-proof alcohol. Every French wine-making region bottles *marc*, but the reputation of Burgundy wines makes *marc de Bourgogne* one of the best known and most widely available *marcs*, both in France and abroad. *Marc* can be quite reasonably priced in regions where it is made, but it tends to be expensive in North American liquor stores and bars. Brandy may be used as a substitute in cooking.

While Frenchmen seem to take special delight in pronouncing *marc* with the most guttural of prolonged gargles, my cyclists often mistakenly pronounce the *c* as well as end their evenings with a *marc* too many. *Marc*, after all, is only slightly less mind-numbing than Italy's *grappa!*

Cod Fillets in a Bath of Brandy and Aligoté Wine

∽

I don't think I've ever traveled in an area that celebrates its fresh-water fish like Burgundy does. As a New England island-dweller accustomed for years to eating fresh saltwater species, I must admiringly confess that I find Burgundians to be brilliant masters of fish cookery. Wines, both red and white, play a vital role in saucing the likes of pike, whitebait, perch, carp, and trout, but in the end the recipe always seems to taste refreshingly light.

Brochet cooked with Aligoté wine—Aligoté being the only other white wine grape besides chardonnay permitted to be grown in the Côte d'Or—is a popular Burgundy recipe and one of my favorites. Back home, I substitute cod fillets for the Burgundian *brochet* to achieve comparably excellent results.

3 tablespoons olive oil
2 pounds cod fillets
3 large shallots, minced
¼ cup minced fresh chives
¼ cup minced fresh parsley
1½ cups Aligoté or other dry white wine
⅓ cup marc de Bourgogne or brandy
Salt and freshly ground black pepper to taste
¼ cup crème fraîche or heavy (or whipping) cream

1. At least 6 hours (and up to 24 hours) ahead of cooking time marinate the cod fillets: Drizzle the olive oil over the bottom of a 13 x 9-inch nonreactive baking dish. Place the cod fillets in the dish

and sprinkle them with the minced shallots, chives, and parsley. Pour the wine and *marc* or brandy over all, cover, and let marinate in the refrigerator for at least 6 hours.

2. Take the cod out of the refrigerator an hour before cooking to let it come to room temperature. Preheat the oven to 425°F.

3. Season the cod fillets with salt and pepper and bake, spooning the pan juices over the top of the fish occasionally, until the fish is just cooked through, 12 to 15 minutes. Turn on the broiler and brush each cod fillet lightly all over with 2 tablespoons of the crème fraîche or heavy cream. Broil the fish 4 to 5 inches away from the heat until lightly glazed on top, 2 to 3 minutes. Serve at once, spooning any remaining pan juices over the top of the fish.

MAKES 4 SERVINGS

Frogs' Legs with Pouilly Fuissé and Parsley

The last time I dined on frogs' legs in France was in Tournus, one of my favorite towns in Burgundy. I love its pretty pink Abbey of St.-Philibert, its fine restaurants, and uniquely romantic lodgings. While Restaurant Greuze tops my Tournus list of eateries, I recently dined finely and more rustically at a little restaurant called Le Voleur de Temps. There, the frogs' legs were given the whimsical name "dancers of the prairie" and were flambéed with pastis. I have adapted the recipe to make it less Provençal and more Burgundian by eliminating the pastis and flavoring the

dish more subtly with Pouilly Fuissé, a dry, golden-green wine rumored to get its famous flavor from the 25,000-year-old bones of horses and reindeer that were discovered buried underneath the vineyards surrounding the Rock of Solutré.

36 pairs medium frogs' legs (usually available frozen
   in selected specialty food stores)
3 tablespoons unbleached all-purpose flour
Sea or coarse salt and freshly ground black pepper to taste
2 tablespoons unsalted butter
2 tablespoons vegetable oil
1½ cups chardonnay wine, preferably Pouilly Fuissé
2 shallots, minced
3 cloves garlic, minced
1 cup crème fraîche
¾ cup minced fresh parsley

1. Thaw the frogs' legs, if frozen, by leaving them in the refrigerator overnight. Pat them dry. Sprinkle them lightly with the flour and then season with salt and pepper.

2. Heat the butter and oil together in a large skillet over medium heat. Add the frogs' legs and sauté for 5 minutes. Add the wine, shallots, and garlic and simmer until the frogs' legs are tender, 15 to 20 minutes. Using a slotted spatula, transfer the frogs' legs to a platter and keep warm.

3. Bring the cooking liquid in the skillet to a boil and cook until reduced by half, 7 to 10 minutes. Add the crème fraîche and continue boiling the mixture until it is thick enough to coat the back of a spoon and reduced by about half, about 10 minutes. Return the frogs' legs to the pan and stir to coat with the sauce. Adjust the seasoning, if necessary, and then stir in the parsley. Serve at once.

MAKES 4 TO 6 SERVINGS

REMEMBRANCE OF

CYCLING
ROUTES PAST

In recent years, Burgundy bicycle trips have come to concentrate on the vineyards and villages of the Côte d'Or, but the
first few trips I guided in the mid-1980s spanned from Dijon to
Romanèche-Thorins, Georges Duboeuf's stomping ground
in Beaujolais. The routes have changed, because there are no
longer the special hotels to accommodate our groups, but the
memories of those early days linger long.

After leaving the southern Côte d'Or, our night's stopover
in Tournus brought exquisite dining at Restaurant Greuze, whose
master chef, Jean Ducloux, began his culinary apprenticeship at
the tender age of thirteen in the kitchens of Dijon's legendary
Restaurant Les Trois Faisins. (M.F.K. Fisher wrote wonderful
descriptions of dining in the 1920s at Les Trois Faisins in *Long
Ago in France—The Years in Dijon.*)

A tour of the town's chief attraction, the pink stone, twin-
towered Abbaye St.-Philibert served as a perfect introduction to
Burgundy's Romanesque trail, for the following day's route led
us through the gentle, green Mâconnais hills toward Cluny and
the surviving ruins of what was once the largest and most powerful monastery in all of Christendom.

Fortified with picnic fare purchased in the early morning

hours from the small markets that line Tournus's medieval streets, we cyclists couldn't help but feel like the twelfth-century pilgrims who had once traveled similar routes past rural churches in growing anticipation of their arrival at the magnificent abbey church at Cluny.

From Cluny, our heads filled with the echoes of imagined Gregorian chants sung over hundreds of years, we pedaled South, past the red tiled roofs of Mâcon even farther back in history to an equally imposing site—the craggy limestone silhouette of the Rock of Solutré. Not content merely to gaze upon this important archaeological site, where 25,000-year-old bones of horses and reindeer have been discovered, our indefatigable group ended the day with a sunset climb to the top of the rock, further crowned by celebratory toasts poured from bottles of chilled Pouilly Fuissé hailing from the vineyards that stretched beneath us. Solutré boasted no elegant château-converted hotel and we stayed instead in a sprawling youth-hostel type complex. No one seemed to mind, since a refreshingly rustic, family-style meal kept everybody reveling around one long, candle-lit table into the wee hours of the morning. To this day, I hold dear vivid memories of the passing of platters of crispy French fries followed, strangely enough, by cozy, midnight philosophizing with cigar-smoking Texans, investment bankers, and idealistic co-guides. These were youthful times lived to the fullest at Solutré's now defunct lodgings. Come morning, Beaujolais and more bicycling beckoned...

REAL MUSTARD

*I*t is not by accident that the word *Dijon* has long had only one association in my one-track culinary mind: mustard! Mustard first became highly regarded in the twelfth and thirteenth centuries, and in Europe it was only produced in Dijon, where the methods used by the Gauls were employed. In 1634, the city of Dijon imposed the first regulations to protect their unique mustard-making trade, though it was not until the eighteenth century and the discovery of combining *verjus* (acidic juice from underripe Burgundy grapes) with brown mustard seeds that Dijon mustard began to earn its worldwide reputation for superior quality. We may think that we have a lot of varieties of mustard on the market today, but mustard was truly all the rage back in the eighteenth and nineteenth centuries, when it was purchased daily in fancy porcelain pots in umpteen flavors, including rose, anchovy, and truffle.

Although Dijon continues to produce about 70 percent of France's mustard, the best and most pungent mustard I've ever tasted is made down the road, in Beaune, at Edmond Fallot. I love this mustard so much that I even toured the factory to check out the ancient production methods. The flint millstones that grind the mustard seeds turn slowly so as not to destroy the fiery flavor of the heat-sensitive seeds. Fallot's mustard is sold all over the Côte d'Or and in the large Casino supermarket chain. Although some Williams-Sonoma stores are now stocking it stateside, I can only advise that if you love mustard don't leave France without Fallot.

Readers should note that all the recipes in this book call for *imported* Dijon mustard. America's Grey Poupon "Dijon" mustard may have great advertisements, but I don't feel it compares in pungency to mustards imported from France. Dessaux, Corcellet, and Maille are all French brands imported into this country that I recommend, if you haven't managed to secure the Fallot brand.

Dijon Deviled Chicken

S ince I have personal and positive feelings about all the recipes
I select for my cookbooks, I'm reluctant to claim a favorite,
but I just can't contain my enthusiasm when it comes to this one.
Here is a super-looking and tasting chicken that's a cinch to make.
It is one that I never cease to crave, no matter how many times
I cook it.

The proper French name for the recipe is *poulet grillé en crapaudine*—*en crapaudine* signifying any bird that has been butterflied and flattened to look like a run-over toad—perhaps not a
very pleasant thought if you are on a bicycle but a very wonderful one indeed if you are about to sit down to this dinner.
Broiling the flattened chicken makes for an extra-crisp yet juicy
bird, and a generous surface smear of extra-sharp Dijon mustard
during the last 2 minutes of cooking ensures that the fiery flavor
and color of the mustard remains intact. The chicken should be
garnished simply, with a smattering of minced fresh herbs from
the garden or windowsill—parsley, chervil, chives, and tarragon
all work well. Add a side of Montrachet Mashed Potatoes (page
84), a bottle of *Cru* Beaujolais, and a refreshing green salad after-

ward, and you're sure to be singing *Vive la France! Vive le poulet! Vive la moutarde!*

> 2 young chickens (about 3 pounds each), butterflied
>   and backbones removed
> ½ cup fresh lemon juice
> ⅓ cup fruity olive oil
> Sea or coarse salt and freshly ground pepper to taste
> 4 to 5 heaping tablespoons imported extra-sharp Dijon mustard
> ½ cup mixed minced fresh herbs, such as parsley,
>   chervil, chives, and tarragon

1. Lay the butterflied chickens, skin side up, on a work surface. Using the heel of your hand, press down on the breast bones to crack them and further flatten the birds. Tuck the wing tips behind the shoulders. Place the birds in a large glass baking dish and drizzle them with the lemon juice and olive oil. Marinate at room temperature for 1 hour.

2. Preheat the broiler.

3. Transfer the chickens, skin side up, to a large roasting rack with a drip pan underneath. Season them with salt and pepper. Broil, 5 inches away from the heat, until the skin is evenly browned and even slightly charred, about 15 minutes. Using tongs, turn the birds and cook the undersides until well browned and slightly charred, another 15 minutes.

4. Remove the chickens from the broiler. Using tongs, turn them one last time so that they are skin side up. Smear the surface of the birds evenly with the mustard. Return to the broiler to brown the mustard until it forms a crust, 2 to 3 minutes. To serve, split the chickens in half, place a half on each of 4 serving plates, sprinkle with the herbs, and enjoy as soon as possible.

MAKES 4 SERVINGS

Coq au Vin Blanc

When I was a teenager, *coq au vin* was one of the first fancy and foreign-sounding dishes I learned to cook. Since, I have made *beaucoup de coqs au vin*, but now I react to the famous dish with more dismay than delight. I guess I've sampled too many indifferent or dubious *coqs au vin* in Burgundy served up as *plats du jour* and have grown to dislike the way the red cooking wine stains the chicken meat an unpalatable brownish gray.

Switch the cooking wine from red to white, but add a good bottle of red Burgundy rather than white as a sipping accompaniment, and suddenly you have one happy *coq au vin* camper. It is not really a sacrilege, as there are plenty of lesser known Burgundian recipes that call for stewing a chicken in white wine. In fact, the one here is adapted from the recipe brochure distributed at the charming Moutarde Grey Poupon boutique in Dijon.

3 tablespoons unsalted butter, softened
2 tablespoons vegetable or olive oil
3 whole chicken breasts (3 to 3½ pounds total), split in half
Sea or coarse salt and freshly ground black pepper to taste
3 cloves garlic, minced
3 shallots, minced
1½ teaspoons dried thyme
1 teaspoon ground marjoram
¾ cup chicken stock, preferably homemade
2 cups white Burgundy table wine, or other chardonnay
½ pound baby carrots, peeled
24 pearl onions, peeled
1 can (13 ounces) artichoke hearts, drained
⅓ cup imported Dijon mustard
3 tablespoons brandy
1 tablespoon unbleached all-purpose flour
½ cup snipped fresh chives or minced fresh parsley

112

1. Heat 2 tablespoons of the butter and the oil in a very large skillet or Dutch oven over medium-high heat. Add the chicken breasts, skin side down, and sauté until nicely browned, 8 to 10 minutes. Season the chicken with salt and pepper while it cooks. Turn over and brown the undersides as well. Once browned, move the chicken breasts to a platter.

2. Add the garlic and shallots to the skillet and sauté until softened, 2 to 3 minutes. Add the thyme and the marjoram and cook 1 minute more. Pour in the chicken stock and wine, stirring to scrape up any browned bits that may be clinging to the bottom of the pan. Return the chicken to the pot, cover, and braise over medium heat, basting occasionally with the pan juices, until the meat is nearly tender, 25 to 30 minutes. Add the carrots, onions, and artichokes, tucking them in and around the chicken pieces, and continue cooking, covered, until the vegetables are tender, 15 to 20 minutes more.

3. Using a slotted spoon, transfer the chicken and vegetables to a platter and keep warm. Whisk the mustard and brandy into the liquid remaining in the skillet and bring to a boil. Using your fingers or a fork, knead the remaining 1 tablespoon butter into the flour until thoroughly combined to make a *beurre manié*. Whisk the *beurre manié* slowly, half-teaspoon by half-teaspoon, into the sauce to slightly thicken it. Taste and add more salt and pepper, if necessary. Return the chicken and vegetables to the pot and stir to coat with the sauce. Sprinkle with the chives or parsley and serve at once.

MAKES 6 SERVINGS

Duck pour Deux

The fertile Bresse country southeast of Mâcon is famed the world over for its pampered, free-range *poulet de Bresse*, known as both "the king of chickens" and "the chicken of kings." On my last Bresse outing, I discovered the lovely Restaurant Lea in the village of Montrevel-en-Bresse, and despite the suggestive and whimsical collection of chickens perched atop Lea's sideboard, I found myself opting instead for the restaurant's sublime way with duckling.

After I swooned over the depth of rosemary essence in the sauce, pooled elegantly about my rosy slices of roasted duck breast, the pleasingly plump Madame Marie-Claude Monnier cheerfully invited me back into the kitchen to meet her husband, chef Louis Monnier. Over two quick infusions of dark-roasted and thick French coffee, Monsieur Monnier revealed to me the secrets of his *poitrine de canette rotie-jus au romarin*. Since I have happily discovered back in my own kitchen that this delicious duck really isn't that difficult to make considering its seductive flavor, I'm inclined to suggest it as a perfect choice for a romantic evening *à deux*. Accompany either with Delicious White Beans (page 82) or Montrachet Mashed Potatoes (page 84).

2 boneless duck breasts (8 to 10 ounces each)
Sea or coarse salt and freshly ground black pepper to taste
1 large shallot, minced
1 small carrot, peeled and minced
2 tablespoons dried rosemary
1 cup Homemade Beef Stock (page 27)
2 tablespoons unsalted butter

1. Preheat the oven to 450°F.

2. Place the duck breasts, skin side up, in a small roasting pan. Season them generously with salt and pepper.

3. Roast the breasts until the skin has browned and begun to crisp, 7 to 8 minutes. After the first 5 minutes of cooking, scatter the minced shallot, carrots, and rosemary around the roasting breasts. Turn the breasts over and roast meat side up for another 4 to 5 minutes to yield rare to medium-rare meat.

4. Remove the duck breasts from the pan and keep warm while making the sauce. To make the sauce, pour the stock into the roasting pan and place over medium-high heat. Stir to scrape up any browned bits clinging to the bottom of the pan and cook until the liquid is reduced by half, 5 to 7 minutes. Strain the mixture through a fine sieve into a small saucepan and discard the solids. Place the saucepan over very low heat and swirl in the butter, a tablespoon at a time, just until melted. Correct the flavor of the sauce with additional salt and pepper, if necessary.

5. Slice the duck breasts on the diagonal into thin slices. Fan the slices onto 2 warmed serving plates and pool the sauce generously over them. Serve at once.

MAKES 2 SERVINGS

Spring Rabbit with Mustard and Cornichons

I call this recipe Spring Rabbit, not because it must be served in the springtime or because it is vital that the rabbit be of spring breeding, but because it took me two visits to Burgundy over separate springtimes to get the recipe exactly right. In March of 1993, my Burgundy neighbor and culinary confidante, Chantal Leroux, quite noticeably beamed when describing to me her recipe for *lapin à la moutarde*. I jotted down some rough bilingual notes and can remember thinking that her recipe sounded not only better but easier than those that I had spied in a bevy of classic Burgundian cookbooks.

When, in a few months' time, I got around to trying to make sense of my notes and prepare the recipe, I knew at once that my rendition was decent but not as worthy of the glow that I could still vividly recall on Chantal's face.

A two-day passage through Beaune the following spring found me planning an apéritif with Chantal as one last opportunity to

take notes anew with the hope of truly perfecting this rabbit recipe. This time around, upon my return home I made Chantal's recipe "quick as a bunny" and at last succeeded in replicating a rabbit dish that I surely would be delighted to serve year-round.

2½ cups fresh bread crumbs
3 tablespoons imported Dijon mustard
⅓ cup minced fresh parsley
3½ tablespoons olive oil
Sea or coarse salt and freshly ground black pepper to taste
2 small rabbits (1½ to 2 pounds each), cut into serving pieces
1 cup heavy (or whipping) cream
1 tablespoon white wine vinegar
5 cornichons, minced

1. Preheat the oven to 350°F.

2. Place the bread crumbs, mustard, parsley, and olive oil in a food processor; process to combine. Season the crumbs with salt and pepper. Arrange the rabbit pieces in a roasting pan in a single layer. Pat them evenly all over with the crumb mixture, and bake until the rabbit is tender and the crumb coating a crisp golden brown, 45 minutes to 1 hour.

3. Transfer the cooked rabbit to a platter and keep warm. Pour the cream and vinegar into the roasting pan and bring it to a boil over medium heat, stirring to scrape up the browned bits clinging to the pan. Stir in the cornichons and continue cooking until the sauce is thick enough to coat the back of a spoon, 4 to 5 minutes more. Pour the sauce over the rabbit and serve at once.

MAKES 4 TO 6 SERVINGS

Note: If the rabbit is for a picnic, the sauce may be eliminated and the crumb-coated rabbit served as is at room temperature.

PORK

OF COURSE!

Spiced Pork Loin

Beaujolais

Sausages & Grapes

Burgundians have been known to carry on unresolvable debates over the art of viticulture for decades on end. Yet when it comes to pinpointing the ingredients that form the foundation of their rich cuisine, there seems to be unanimous agreement on these four: wine, cream, pork, and pastry. The recipes in this chapter encompass three out of the four, but mostly they give a Gallic twist to the American idea of bringing home the bacon.

Baked Fresh Ham "Grand-Mère"

As one who has benefited enormously from recipes handed down to me from both my maternal and paternal grandmothers, I instinctively gravitate to any French recipe or menu item with *grand-mère* in the title. Most *grand-mère* recipes burst with rich and homey flavors from long and slow roasting, yielding old-fashioned and simple cooked comforts in this fast-paced culinary age of flash-searing, stir-fries, and sushi.

As I have mentioned before, pork in myriad forms is a cornerstone of Burgundian cooking, and there is no better and more aromatic lazy Sunday dinner fare than this fresh ham, baked languorously over the course of an entire afternoon with plenty of garlic, savory herbs, and white wine.

6 cloves garlic, minced
1 bunch scallions, trimmed and minced
1 cup minced fresh parsley
½ cup minced fresh chives
½ cup minced fresh sage
½ cup minced fresh rosemary
1 fresh ham (8 to 10 pounds), trimmed of all but a
    thin layer of surface fat
Sea or coarse salt and freshly ground black pepper
    to taste
2 cups dry white Burgundy wine or other
    chardonnay

119

1. Preheat the oven to 350°F.

2. Place the garlic, scallions, parsley, chives, sage, and rosemary in a food processor. Process them all together until almost pastelike in consistency.

3. Using a small sharp knife, make several 2-inch-deep slits all over the fresh ham. With your hands, stuff half of the herb blend into the slits and pat lightly over the surface of the ham.

Reserve the remaining half for later use. Place the ham, fat side up, in a roasting pan and sprinkle it all over with the salt and pepper.

4. Bake the ham, uncovered, for 1½ hours. Reduce the oven temperature to 325°F, add the wine to the roasting pan, and continue to bake, uncovered, for another hour, basting occasionally. Pat the remaining half of the herb blend all over the ham, cover the pan tightly with foil, and continue roasting for another 2 hours. Baste the ham occasionally with the pan juices. At the end of 4½ hours of cooking, the ham should be very tender and almost falling off the bone.

5. Transfer the ham to a carving platter and let it rest, loosely covered, for 10 to 15 minutes. Meanwhile, skim off and discard any fat from the liquid in the roasting pan. Pour the remaining juices into a small saucepan and keep warm over low heat. Carve the ham into ½-inch-thick slices and serve moistened with the warm pan juices.

MAKES 8 TO 10 SERVINGS

....

GREAT BEAUJOLAIS is always an exhilarating drink. It's as clean, direct, and effusive an expression of a grape as you're apt to find in all of winedom. Uncork a good example of Beaujolais and the adjectives flit past. What other wine suggests crunchy red fruit, violets, peonies, strawberries, raspberries, plums, cherries, peaches, and bananas—in a single, swift slurp?

—DAVID ROSENGARTEN
THE WINE & FOOD COMPANION

....

Spiced Pork Loin with Beaujolais-Soused Bing Cherries

During the March I spent gathering recipes for this book in a little house perched on *la Montagne de Beaune,* my neighbor, Chantal, generously shared companionship and culinary wisdom with me. She lent me all her favorite cookbooks, including a glorious, just-published one called *Colette Gourmande.* As we both shared a love for Colette's writing, we relished the opportunity to savor her delicious words and food together. When I was leaving France, I picked up a current issue of the food magazine *Saveurs,* which coincidentally featured a beautifully illustrated article on the gastronomic enchantments of Colette's Burgundy birthplace—La Puisaye. An exquisite photo of a fresh cherry soup that was supposedly prepared on days when "one didn't cook" *chez* Collette put me in the mood to do something Burgundian with cherries. It was with impatience that I waited for cherry season to come to New England so that I could cook this pork loin—a recipe jotted down from another of Chantal's Burgundy cookbooks.

PORK

1 pork loin (approximately 4 pounds), trimmed of
    all but a very thin layer of surface fat
2 teaspoons mixed (pink, green, black, and
    white) whole peppercorns
20 whole cloves
1 tablespoon ground cinnamon
6 tablespoons (¾ stick) unsalted butter, at room
    temperature
Sea or coarse salt to taste
1 large onion, coarsely chopped
½ to 1 cup red Beaujolais wine

CHERRY SAUCE

1½ pounds pitted Bing cherries
2 tablespoons light brown sugar
2 tablespoons balsamic vinegar
3 tablespoons fresh rosemary, coarsely chopped
1½ cups Beaujolais wine

FINISHING

⅓ cup plus 2 tablespoons kirsch or other cherry-flavored
    eau de vie
2 tablespoons cornstarch dissolved in 3 tablespoons
    Beaujolais wine

1. Preheat the oven to 375°F. Bring the pork loin to room temperature.

2. Combine the peppercorns, 10 of the cloves, and the cinnamon and use a mortar and pestle or small spice grinder to pound or grind them into a coarse powder. Blend together the spices and softened butter to make a paste. With a small sharp knife, make

random ½-inch-deep incisions in 10 spots on the pork loin; insert the remaining 10 cloves. Smear the pork all over with the spiced butter and sprinkle with sea salt. Scatter the chopped onion over the bottom of a flameproof roasting pan and place the pork loin on top. Pour ½ cup of Beaujolais into the bottom of the pan.

3. Roast the pork, basting occasionally with the wine and accumulated pan juices, until a meat thermometer inserted in the center

of the roast reads at least 160°F, 1½ to 1¾ hours. Add more Beaujolais if the bottom of the roasting pan is becoming too dry.

4. Meanwhile, make the cherry sauce: Place the cherries, brown sugar, balsamic vinegar, rosemary, and 1½ cups Beaujolais wine in a large saucepan. Bring to a boil and then simmer, uncovered, stirring occasionally, for 20 minutes.

5. When the pork is fully cooked, pour ⅓ cup of the kirsch over it, and using caution (stand back and make sure nothing flammable is nearby), light a match and flambé the roast in the pan. When the flames subside, transfer the pork loin to a platter and keep warm in a low oven. Stir the remaining 2 tablespoons kirsch into the cherry sauce.

6. Place the roasting pan on a burner over medium heat. Stir in the dissolved cornstarch and cook to thicken the pan juices. Pour the cherry sauce into the roasting pan and continue to cook until all is blended and slightly thickened, 4 to 5 minutes more.

7. Carve the pork into ½-inch-thick slices, arrange on a large serving platter, and surround generously with the cherry sauce. Serve at once.

MAKES 6 TO 8 SERVINGS

123

Mignonettes of Pork à l'Ancienne

How can anyone not like a restaurant with an address on rue Paradis and a signature dish of succulent sautéed pork strips in a classic old-fashioned cream and mustard sauce? No wonder Beaune's Restaurant des Arts Deco and its *mignonettes de porc à l'ancienne* are favorites in my cycling crowd. While the richness of this dish might best be savored after a vigorous day of Hautes-Côtes biking, it shouldn't be missed, as it is one of the few irresistible and oh-so-Burgundian recipes that's easy to make. Tender strips of beef, and even chicken or turkey, may be substituted for the pork, if desired. Serve with a simple accompaniment, such as white rice.

2 pounds lean pork tenderloin
2 tablespoons unsalted butter
1 tablespoon vegetable oil
3 shallots, minced
½ cup dry white vermouth
1¼ cups heavy (or whipping) cream
3 tablespoons imported coarse-grained Dijon mustard
Sea or coarse salt and freshly ground black pepper
½ cup minced fresh parsley

1. Cut the pork into thin strips 2 inches long and ½ inch wide. Pat them dry with paper towels.

2. Heat the butter and oil in a large skillet over medium-high heat. Sauté the pork in batches until seared on all sides and just

cooked through the center, 5 to 7 minutes per batch. Transfer to a platter and keep warm.

3. Add the shallots to the skillet and sauté for 2 minutes. Pour in the vermouth, bring to a boil, and cook until reduced by half, 3 to 5 minutes. Add the cream and blend in 1½ tablespoons of the mustard; continue cooking and reducing until the sauce is thick enough to coat the back of a spoon, 7 to 8 minutes. Swirl in the remaining 1½ tablespoons mustard and season the sauce to taste with salt and pepper. Return the pork strips to the pan and stir to coat with the sauce. Sprinkle in the parsley just before serving and serve immediately.

MAKES 4 TO 6 SERVINGS

125

Sausages with White Wine and Green Grapes

This is my adaptation of a rustic dish popular around the south of Burgundy, in the rolling Beaujolais hills. There the dish is known as *andouillette vigneronne*—andouillette is a tripe sausage for which I have yet to acquire a taste, though it is beloved by the locals. I do, however, have a fondness for anything *vigneronne*—usually indicating that grapes and/or wine will be used in the cooking. In the following rendition, easy-to-find sweet Italian sausages pair harmoniously with the more traditional French ingredients. But if you take the extra effort to seek out different kinds

of freshly made sausages from an artisan sausage maker, such as San Franciscan Bruce Aidells (his are sold in many specialty food stores around the country), you'll feel especially rewarded.

> 8 fresh sausages (about 1½ pounds), such as sweet Italian
> 2 tablespoons unsalted butter, for greasing gratin dish
> 3 shallots, minced
> 1½ cups dry white Burgundy wine or other chardonnay
> 2 to 3 tablespoons imported Dijon mustard
> 1 cup seedless green grapes, halved
> Sea or coarse salt and freshly ground black pepper to taste
> 3 tablespoons minced fresh parsley

1. Place the sausages in a large skillet, cover with water, and bring to a boil over medium-high heat. Simmer, uncovered, until the sausages are no longer pink inside, 12 to 15 minutes. Drain.

2. Preheat the oven to 425°F.

3. Generously butter the bottom of a shallow flameproof 1-quart gratin dish. Sprinkle the shallots over the bottom and arrange the drained sausages on top. Pour the wine over all.

4. Bake the sausages, turning them several times so that they brown all over. This usually takes 35 to 40 minutes, during which about half the wine will evaporate.

5. Remove the cooked sausages from the gratin dish and keep warm. Place the gratin dish on top of a burner over medium-low heat. Swirl in the mustard—2 tablespoons for a milder sauce and 3 for a pronounced mustard flavor. Add the grapes and continue to cook until the grapes are heated through. Season the sauce with salt and pepper. Place the sausages on a platter, nap generously with the mustard-grape sauce, sprinkle with the minced parsley, and serve at once.

MAKES 4 SERVINGS

A PERSONAL BEST OF
BEAUNE

Study any number of travel guidebooks devoted to Burgundy, and you will be informed, in similar phrases, that Beaune has a population of roughly 22,000 people and is the

center of both the wine and tourist trade in the Côte d'Or. Located 192 miles south of Paris, Beaune is geographically situated in the heart of France. It is one of the country's most visited and admired small medieval cities. As might well be expected of a quaint French destination, the town itself is chock-full of history, hotels, restaurants, and shops—many of which specialize in the region's exceptional wines along with decorative drinking and serving accoutrements.

More romantic, locally published guides describe Beaune as a secretive and mysterious place and often begin by describing a jewel of a town where "the cicadas sing in the warm summer and Roman tiles are not uncommon. Three winds blow across the region, breathing life into it: the cold North wind;

the warm South wind, which sometimes carries sand from Africa, and the wind of the Morvan, a westerly wind that brings rain and often storms. The vegetation all around thrives on these three airstreams and the vine flourishes, to give 'the finest wines in Christendom.'"

Facts and fabrications aside, or perhaps combined, Beaune has always been particularly alluring to me because it so often reminds me of the New England island of Nantucket, which I call home. It might appear to be quite a stretch to compare a place layered in history spanning a gamut from Caesar to Charlemagne and from ascetic medieval convent life to the grandeur of the Capetian and Valois dukes with an American island touched by a mere few hundred years of history. But I simply cannot deny feeling the existence of many present-day similarities. Both Beaune and Nantucket are living and functioning historical places, as opposed to reconstructed museum theme parks. Both entice numerous visitors and tourists who enjoy serene strolls along cobblestoned streets lined with beautifully preserved old houses brightened by windowsill and garden cascades of well-tended flowers. Both are laden with unique restaurants, hotels, and shops that invite comparisons and make for a focal point of life and conversation in the town. And, finally, the self-contained nature of both Beaune and Nantucket breeds an intimacy that can be as welcoming as it is infuriating. As for drawing parallels between an ocean-fringed island and a land-locked town, Beaune, as any visitor will inevitably discover, virtually floats on a labyrinth of underground cellars housing tens of thousands of bottles of wine. That ancient Greek notion of "a wine-dark sea" completes the imagery for me, and thereby qualifies Beaune, like Nantucket, as an island unto itself.

Beaune serves as the cultural anchor of the bicycle trips I lead in Burgundy, and over the years I have developed the following subjective list of Beaune-based favorites, and learned that it is indeed accurately stated that "Beaune, like its wine, should be tasted with love."

HISTORIC BEAUNE

After a few days of biking through rural Burgundy vineyards, which stretch as far as the eye can see, meandering around Beaune on foot brings welcome contrast. I love taking early-morning and late-night after-dinner strolls along the town's old walls, or *remparts*. Gazing up at harmoniously diverse rooftops, peering into quiet little courtyards, and imagining life behind the imposing iron gates of many a wine merchant's mansion never

fails to yield private insights and aesthetic gratifications not gleaned from the more trodden tours of Beaune's better-known historical monuments.

Still, I must advise that the Hôtel-Dieu, Beaune's chief tourist attraction and one that receives more than 350,000 visitors a year, is not to be missed. Built in the flamboyant Gothic style by marrying local Burgundian building tradition with rich Flemish artistry, the Hôtel-Dieu was founded in 1443 by Nicolas Rolin and his third wife, Guigone de Salins, as a medieval hospital "where the poor and sick were provided with everything necessary for their relief." So splendid and rich in symbols is this hospice that I can enthusiastically visit it time and again and readily understand why the local Beaunois call it the "eighth wonder of the world." I never cease to marvel at the way the

massive and solemn gray exterior of the hospital belies an open, airy inner courtyard with a dazzling roof of yellow, red, green, and black varnished Flemish tiles.

The magnificent hall for the sick, the *Salle des Pôvres,* with its pastel ornamented and beamed ceiling built to resemble the upside-down hull of a Viking ship and the stage-set lineup of elegant beds draped in rich red fabric, almost makes me wish I were sick and poor and living in medieval Beaune. However, a few minutes of gazing at the Flemish polyptych of anguished souls depicted in the painting of the Last Judgment, which originally hung on the high altar of the *Salle des Pôvres,* is always enough to jar me back to reality and make me happy to be healthily pedaling my way about the Burgundian countryside in the twentieth century.

For some, a morning or afternoon tour of the Hôtel-Dieu will serve as sufficient sightseeing, but those keen on art and architecture will certainly want to take a five-minute walk north to view the appealing mix of Romanesque, Gothic, and Renaissance elements in the Church of Notre Dame. Be sure to check out the side presbytery, lovely turret, and peaceful private garden, which was home to Guigone de Salins for seven years.

Since so much of Beaune is tied to the wine industry, I also highly recommend a visit to the nearby Musée du Vin, housed in a former ducal palace. A collection of old wine presses, in-depth insight into the distinctly Burgundian notion of *terroir,* and artifacts that trace the history of wine since ancient times to the beginning of the twentieth century can all be absorbed in a visit of about an hour.

SHOPPING

If you are passionate about wine, food, and unique gastronomic gadgetry, then Beaune will most likely seem like par-
adise found. The Athenaeum de la Vigne et du Vin, with
entrances both on the main Place Carnot and down from the
central tourist office, is by far my favorite store in Beaune. I
could while away all my hours and francs in this sprawling
emporium filled with fabulous books, regional and global, on
food and wine, written in both French and English. There's
even a cozy wine-tasting bar and two rooms displaying wines
for sale from the cellars of the shop's owner, Patriarche Père
et Fils, who claims to have "*les plus grandes caves de la Bourgogne.*" The Athenaeum is also a good place to purchase wine
maps, unique cards, and regional guidebooks. Informative videos
on wine are frequently shown upstairs in the Athenaeum alongside rooms with changing historical exhibitions.

Denis Perret, Moillard, and Yves Clement are three elegant
wine stores filled with hundreds of wines from Burgundy, dis-

played with a care usually accorded precious jewels. While there are *Grand Cru* wines that can easily run 200 dollars a bottle, bargains may also be had, like the delicious Beaujolais Nouveau of Yves Clement for a mere 4 dollars a bottle. These stores are all located on or near place Carnot as you head toward the tourist office.

If the thought of parting with upwards of 800 francs for a fine bottle of Burgundy leaves you faint, then perhaps a *Grand Cru* bottle in the form of a miniature refrigerator magnet can fill the souvenir bill as well as please the pocketbook. The diminutive bottle of Bâtard-Montrachet that graces my refrigerator's exterior never fails to be a conversation piece. The magnets cost a few dollars, and a prodigious assortment of them may be found at Laronze Droguerie, 7 place Carnot.

Another fun store for wine-related paraphernalia is Le Vigneron, at 6 rue d'Alsace. This is the place to buy shiny silver Burgundy wine-tasting cups, called *tastevins,* wine glasses with Côte d'Or insignias, gold-plated grape leaves, champagne sabers, unusual corkscrews, and the wonderfully voluptuous, traditional Burgundian grape-picking baskets in an assortment of sizes.

Beaune's bustling pedestrian zone, comprising rues Carnot and Monge, inevitably fuels my quest for Burgundian sundries, both for carrying home and immediate consumption. My first stop is always Geneviève Lethu, a chic tableware and gift shop with locations throughout France. The pale red, cherub-decorated, oversize cups from which I sip my *café au lait* on Sunday mornings were carted carefully home from here. Other Geneviève Lethu favorites include colorful linens, *escargot* dishes in the form of grape clusters, and lots of extraordinary candles molded into fantasy flowers and foods.

At the intersection of rue Monge and rue Carnot is Beaune's best charcuterie, Roger Batteault. There are delicious salads for picnics, fine pâtés, and the only version of *jambon persillé* in all of Burgundy that I've ever been able to abide.

If pork products don't tickle the fancy, then you'll certainly want to opt for the inviting, purple-facaded Biscuiterie Fagot, across the street from the charcuterie. I can never resist buying lots of the very portable and prettily packaged small Burgundian small hard candies known as *Anis de l'Abbaye de Flavigny*. I'm especially fond of the *anis* and *violette* flavors. A few doors up, at 23 rue Carnot, is Le Tast' Fromage, which happens to be my idea of dairy delight. All of Burgundy's finest cheeses are available here at the peak of ripe perfection. The store also has an ample supply of Beaune-made Fallot mustards—the finest mustards in the world, in my opinion.

One may not think of checking out a hardware store in the course of a shopping spree, but I often enjoy a visit to the Quincaillerie Muratier, at 9 rue Carnot, because they carry a large supply of the typically French, blue-enameled number plaques. The number fifteen on the pink front door of my Nantucket home comes from the Quincaillerie Muratier, along with the *"chien lunatique"* plaque that warns visitors of a close friend's crazed Jack Russell terrier.

Continuing up the pedestrian zone, you will appropriately pass through the place au Beurre (butter) before coming to Madame Bouché's sublime pâtisserie, on the place Monge. Nothing ever disappoints here. The *gougères* are crisp and oh-so-cheesy, and the pastries are all as sinfully satisfying as they appear. Two favorite handmade Bouché chocolates to bring back to the United States are *Burgondines*—a crunchy, white sugar-coated almond-shaped candy housing a creamy and rich chocolate-hazelnut center—and assorted foil-wrapped chocolates in the shape of *escargots*. Diagonally across the street from Madame Bouché is the *boulangerie* that all the locals say bakes the best *baguettes* in Beaune. I concur.

WINE TASTING

Places to sample Burgundy wines abound in Beaune, but two that offer unique experiences are the Caves des Cordeliers and Demeure Saint-Martin. The Caves des Cordeliers is just down the street from the Hôtel-Dieu on rue de l'Hôtel-Dieu and is housed in a convent that was inhabited from the beginning of the thirteenth century by an order of monks started by Saint Francis of Assisi. The monks wore tunics of gray cloth tied with a triple-knotted belt made of cord, which in turn gave them their name, *Cordeliers*. Today the upper floor of the refectory houses sisters of the Hôtel-Dieu. Downstairs the wine cellars are open to the public for the unique experience of sampling wines directly from the barrels in which they are aging. The Demeure Saint-Martin is located at 4 boulevard Maréchal Foch, on the outer ring road that circles around the town of Beaune. Here a wine tasting commences with a tour of a beautifully restored eighteenth-century Burgundian residence, replete with Louis XV bedrooms, a rustic kitchen, and an elegant dining room and library. A descent to the wine cellar offers a chance to taste a few wines from the famous Hospices de Beaune wine auction, held in November each year to raise money for charity and thus continue the good deeds of the Hôtel-Dieu.

RESTAURANTS

B eaune and its environs are host to more than 120 eating establishments, and, like those of other restaurant-laden places in the world, these ebb in and out of favor and fashion. Often when I arrive in Beaune, I already have a couple of Michelin-starred dining extravaganzas under my necessarily expandable belt, so I tend to be more in the mood for casual but good dining experiences rather than multicourse decadence.

As it turns out, my very favorite restaurant in Beaune breaks all my normal rules for scouting out a good restaurant. No one whose judgment I trust has ever mentioned it to me; it is located right next to the tourist office and the town's most visited attraction, the Hôtel-Dieu. The restaurant itself is the dining room of the unremarkably named Hôtel Central. I was originally enticed into the restaurant by its walls, which are the rich salmon color of a well-made *sauce Nantua,* and the timbered ceilings, which beckoned with warmth and French charm. Much to my delight, I soon discovered that Restaurant le Central does indeed make a superb *sauce Nantua* to nap its feathery pike *quenelles*. In fact, all the fish I've ordered here tastes exceptional. But what excites me the most about the cooking at le Central is that chef Jean Garcin allows plenty of Provençal influences to seep into what is billed as traditional Burgundian fare everywhere else in town. The last time I dined in the restaurant, I ordered *escargots à la barigoule*, a term designating a light and herby broth, usually paired with artichokes in the south of France. The dish was not only beautiful to behold but even more sensational to savor. In short, I find Restaurant le Central's food truly inspired, the prices reasonable, and the wine list and service excellent. While, admittedly, there's a painting or two I wouldn't want hanging in my dining room, the cumulative effect of fine wine and food tends to transcend all. Restaurant le Central serves both lunch and dinner. The address is 2 rue Victor-Millot.

Another good Beaune bet is Le Gourmandin, an inviting bistro in place Carnot with mirrored walls and handwritten menus. It is run by the highly regarded and ultra-posh Hostellerie de Levernois, located a few miles outside of Beaune, and the in-town food, wine, and atmosphere have a satisfying, rustic polish. However, I've had to forgive surly service upon occasion.

Two friendly restaurants with dependably tasty food are Restaurant des Arts Deco, on rue Paradis, and La Ciboulette, near Porte St.-Nicolas on rue de Lorraine. The former is a cozy restaurant decorated with the proprietor's photographs and is pop-ular for its array of large salads. Main courses change according to the chef's whim and the season. The wine list frequently has some older Burgundies at decent prices. La Ciboulette has an odd decor, which seems more appropriate to Palm Beach than the Côte d'Or. Fortunately, the food is just the reverse, and the place is especially conducive to making new friends. During one cold and desolate March, I ended up sharing the evening with two fellows who turned out to be wine merchants on Nantucket's neighbor-ing island Martha's Vineyard. A small world is always made all the more palatable with a fine meal and copious amounts of incred-ible wines.

Many in Beaune will end an evening on the town with a coffee at either of the two large cafés/brasseries on place Carnot. I don't mind doing as the locals do if weather permits outdoor seating. But, if forced inside, I'd rather go to Pickwick's than suffer the hideous modern interior decor of these other-wise typically French institutions. Pickwick's has an English pub upstairs and a stone-vaulted wine bar downstairs. I prefer the wine bar because it is thankfully nonsmoking and relatively quiet. The wine selection is wonderful to boot. Pickwick's is located at 2 rue Notre-Dame, and as the management likes to say, it is the place to be' when in Beaune.

From the seat of a bicycle, it is easy to figure out how menus for much of Burgundy's traditional cuisine are inspired. If we're not winding through Côte de Nuits villages and vineyards following routes that sound like wine lists in the world's top restaurants, then we're likely to be meandering alongside pastures dotted with Burgundy's prized Charolais cattle. Cycling does indeed make the sensational savor of red Burgundy wine with rich red meats all the more indelible. What better way to select the evening's bottle of red than to order it in honor of the town where, perhaps, you got your first flat tire or turned right rather than left? Shall it be a Nuits-St.-Georges or Chambolle-Musigny to accompany tonight's hearty *boeuf*?

Food writer Roy Andries de Groot penned one of my all-time favorite comments on wine when he declared: "The 'perfect marriage' of food and wine should allow for infidelity." Be as per-fidious as you dare when pairing wines with the robust recipes in this chapter, for it matters not whether the pour is Gevrey-Chambertin or Givry, Morey-St.-Denis or Mercurey, so long as it is red! red! red!

Boeuf Bourguignonne
à Ma Façon

I might as well get right to the point and confess that I've never eaten a dinner of *boeuf bourguignonne* that compelled me to run back into my kitchen and reproduce it. Nonetheless, there is an understandable compulsion among every meat-eating cyclist who visits Burgundy to order this beef and red wine stew in the land that named it. I began to figure that I'd be doing lots of diners as well as myself a favor if I fiddled with the recipe. Fearing also the repercussions of not including Burgundy's most famous recipe in a book devoted to Burgundy-style cooking, I took immediately to the drawing board, or more accurately, to my outdoor grill.

141

Noticing that Burgundians these days seem to be enjoying grilling as much as North Americans, I became inspired to skewer all the traditional *boeuf bourguignonne* ingredients—chunks of beef, bacon, boiling onions, and mushroom caps—and then give them the smoky sear of the outdoor grill, thereby turning a quintessential winter recipe into a great summer one. The skewers are served atop a stove-simmered sauce of red wine and mushrooms, making a traditionally heavy dish lighter and lots of fun, too. Slightly chilled Beaujolais makes a great summer quaff for the feast.

Red Wine and Mushroom Sauce

1 ounce dried mushrooms, preferably cèpes

¾ cup water

5 tablespoons unsalted butter

¾ pound fresh white mushrooms, trimmed and finely
    chopped

1 medium onion, finely chopped

4 cloves garlic, minced

3½ tablespoons unbleached all-purpose flour

1 cup homemade beef stock (page 27) or canned broth

1 cup red Burgundy wine, preferably with 13% alcohol

Sea or coarse salt and freshly ground black pepper to taste

Beef Skewers

½ cup dry mustard

1½ tablespoons coarsely cracked black peppercorns

1 teaspoon sea or coarse salt

3 pounds beef tenderloin, cut into 2-inch cubes

¾ pound sliced bacon, blanched in boiling water for
    1 minute and then drained

24 firm mushroom caps, white or shiitake or a combination
    of the two

18 boiling onions (1½ to 2 inches in diameter), blanched
    in boiling water for 5 minutes, drained, and peeled

½ cup minced fresh parsley

1. Make the red wine and mushroom sauce: Combine the dried mushrooms and water in a small saucepan and bring to a boil. Remove from the heat and let stand for at least 15 minutes.

2. Meanwhile, melt the butter over medium heat in a 10-inch skillet. Add the fresh white mushrooms, onion, and garlic and sauté until quite soft and beginning to brown, 10 to 15 minutes. Stir in

the flour and cook 2 minutes, stirring constantly. Slowly whisk in the beef stock and red wine, stirring to make a smooth sauce. Strain the liquid from the dried mushrooms into the sauce. Mince the dried mushrooms and add them to the sauce. Season the sauce to taste with salt and pepper and simmer for at least 30 minutes to blend the flavors and reduce the sauce slightly. Keep warm.

3. Prepare an outdoor grill for direct and indirect cooking by making a fire on one side of the grill only.

4. Make the beef skewers: Stir together the mustard, pepper-corns, and salt in a small bowl. Rub this mixture lightly all over the beef cubes to season them. Wrap each cube of beef with a strip of bacon, cut to fit. Then thread the beef cubes, alternating with the mushroom caps and onions, on each of 6 metal skewers.

5. Sear the skewers quickly on all sides on the fire side of the grill. Transfer to the nonfire side, cover, and continue cooking indi-rectly until the bacon is crisp, the vegetables tender, and the meat cooked to the desired degree of doneness, about 15 to 20 minutes for medium-rare meat.

6. Serve the skewers atop a generous pool of the red wine and mushroom sauce and sprinkle each serving with some parsley.

MAKES 6 SERVINGS

BURGUNDY 101

To the uninitiated, understanding how Burgundy wines are classified and how these wines, made from only four grape varieties, can vary so much in quality, style, and price, is a daunting task. While I intend for this book to be a cookbook, I recognize that it is impossible to discuss much of anything in Burgundy without relating it to wine. Since there are many terrific books devoted exclusively to Burgundy's wines, I have, not without some difficulty, decided to keep my wine discussions rather general. Thus, here follows the most simplified overview on Burgundy wine of which I am capable.

Just as Caesar wrote "All Gaul is divided into three parts," the first thing to know is that all Burgundy is divided into five wine regions. From north to south, they are Chablis, Côte d'Or, Côte Chalonnais, the Mâconnais, and Beaujolais. Four grapes are permitted to be planted in these areas. Pinot noir and gamay grapes produce red wines, and chardonnay and aligoté grapes produce white wines. The most prized wines in all of Burgundy come from vineyards in the Côte d'Or, planted with pinot noir and chardonnay. Chablis is also known for its minerally *Premier Cru* and *Grand Cru* wines vinified from chardonnay grapes. Aligoté is planted throughout the entire region and produces crisp and dry white wines, considered to be the perfect base for mixing with cassis for an apéritif called a kir. Gamay is the grape of fun and fruity red Beaujolais wines from southern Burgundy.

The wines of the Côte d'Or give Burgundy its world renown,

and it is there that most of my cycling tours are concentrated. Côte d'Or translates literally as "slope of gold," and a vineyard's position on this slope, which is further divided into Côte de Beaune, Côte de Nuits, and Hautes-Côtes, means everything to the wine's classification, or *appellation contrôlée*. Generally, wines labeled *Bourgogne blanc* or *Bourgogne rouge* come from the flat, poorly drained vineyards closest to the RN7 highway, which forms the axis of the Côte d'Or. These are also known as table wines. Wines allowed to bear the name of a particular village, such as Puligny-Montrachet or Volnay, come from the next tier up on the slope.

The most highly regarded wines come from vineyards located about two-thirds of the way up the gradient of the Côte, with southeast exposures to the sun. These are *Premier Cru* and *Grand Cru* vineyards. *Premier Cru* bottles of wine are designated by both the name of the village and the particular vineyard: Meursault Premier Cru, Les Caillerets, for example. *Grand Cru* wines are considered to be so famous that everyone is supposed to know their origin, so only the vineyard's name is printed on the label. Bâtard-Montrachet and Romanée-Conti are two classic and very expensive *Grand Cru* examples.

Beaujolais wines are ranked similarly according to the vineyard's location on the undulating hills of that happy landscape: Beaujolais, Beaujolais-Villages, and *Cru* Beaujolais. *Cru* Beaujolais wines take their names from the ten villages that are deemed to produce the best Beaujolais of the more than one hundred million bottles produced in the area annually. The ten *Crus* are Juliènas, Chénas, Morgon, Moulin-à-Vent, Fleurie, Chiroubles, St.-Amour, Brouilly, Côte-de-Brouilly, and Régnié.

Two favorite books highly recommended for further reading are Kermit Lynch's engaging *Adventures on the Wine Route* and Matt Kramer's *Making Sense of Burgundy*.

Salt-Crusted
Beef Tenderloin

∽

When I think of pairing food with the dreamiest of Burgundy's legendary red wines, I unquestionably favor fabulous red meat preparations. Intrigued by two recipes for a beef tenderloin oven-roasted in the moisture-sealing armor of a salt and flour crust that I had coincidentally seen in diverse places—an ancient (1955) issue of *Gourmet* magazine and the more recently published cookbook *Simply French,* in which Patricia Wells presents the stunning cuisine of Parisian restaurateur Joel Robuchon—I set out to experiment with my own Salt-Crusted Beef Tenderloin. Six very expensive certified Angus tenderloins and *Grand Cru* Côtes de Nuits wines later and just shy of filing for bankruptcy, I can now confidently share my perfected results for the tenderest, rosiest, juiciest, and most flavorful beef tenderloin recipe I know.

146

The recipe is a great one to serve when entertaining, to boot, since the tenderloin is meant to sit in its salt crust for up to an hour after it has been roasted. Depending on the season or the morning's reading on the bathroom scale, accompany the meat with either the Creamy Cognac and Mustard Sauce or somewhat less rich Tomato-Mustard Coulis (recipes follow). And, by all means, don't forget to pour the best red Burgundy you can find and afford.

SALT CRUST
1 cup sea or coarse salt
4 cups unbleached all-purpose flour
1½ tablespoons dried rosemary
2 teaspoons dried thyme
2 large egg whites
¾ to 1¼ cups water

BEEF
1 tablespoon vegetable oil
1 top-quality beef tenderloin, trimmed of fat
    (about 3 pounds after trimming)
1 large clove garlic, cut into thin slivers
¼ cup imported Dijon mustard
2 teaspoons dried tarragon
Freshly ground black pepper to taste
1 large egg yolk beaten with 1 tablespoon water
Creamy Cognac and Mustard Sauce or
        Tomato-Mustard Coulis (recipes follow)

147

1. At least 3 hours ahead of time and up to 24 hours in advance, prepare the salt crust: Stir the salt, flour, rosemary, and thyme together in a large mixing bowl. Make a well in the center and add the egg whites and ¾ cup of the water. Work the liquids into the dry ingredients to make a stiff dough. Add up to ½ cup more water if the dough seems too dry and isn't sticking together. Knead the dough with your hands until it is smooth and homogeneous, 2 to 3 minutes. Cover the dough with plastic wrap and let it rest for a day, if possible. (This makes it easier to roll out.)

2. When ready to cook the meat, preheat the oven to 375°F.

3. Heat the vegetable oil in a large, heavy skillet over medium-high heat. Add the tenderloin and sear it, turning frequently, until lightly browned on all sides. Place the tenderloin on a platter and reserve any drippings in the skillet if you are making the Creamy Cognac and Mustard Sauce to accompany the meat. Using a small and sharp paring knife, make approximately 8 random slits, ½ inch deep, over the surface of the meat. Insert a sliver of garlic into each slit. Spread the mustard evenly all over the top and sides of the tenderloin and then season it by sprinkling with the tarragon and pepper.

4. Roll out the salt crust on a lightly floured surface to form a rough 16 x 12-inch rectangle. Carefully lift the crust and wrap it completely around the tenderloin so that the seam falls underneath the meat. Seal securely and then trim away any excess dough from the ends and seal them securely as well. It is important for everything to be tightly sealed—there should be no gaps in the dough. Rips and tears may be patched if necessary with scraps of dough, which will adhere when moistened with water. Transfer the wrapped tenderloin to a roasting pan. Brush the dough all over with the beaten egg yolk mixture to make a shiny glaze.

5. Roast the tenderloin in the center of the oven. Allow 12 to 15 minutes per pound for rare meat and a few minutes more for medium. An instant-read meat thermometer will guarantee the best results in testing for doneness. For rare meat, the reading should be between 100°F and 110°F and around 125°F for medium. This takes into consideration that the tenderloin will continue to cook as it stands out of the oven in its crust. When the tenderloin has cooked to the desired degree of doneness, let it stand for at least 30 minutes and up to 1 hour before serving. Use that time to prepare either the Creamy Cognac and Mustard Sauce or Tomato-Mustard Coulis.

148

6. To serve, slice open and discard the entire salt crust. Carve the meat into ½-inch slices, spooning any oozing juices over it. Nap the slices of meat with either the Creamy Cognac and Mustard Sauce or the Tomato-Mustard Coulis. Serve at once.

MAKES 6 SERVINGS

CREAMY COGNAC AND
MUSTARD SAUCE

This rich and irresistible sauce is probably as old as any of the oldest surviving vines in Burgundy's most famous vineyards. For me, it embodies the throw-cholesterol-cares-to-the-wind approach of most traditional Burgundy cuisine. But how can anyone resist a sauce with tons of cream, Cognac, and pungent mustard!

149

2 shallots, minced
1 cup Cognac
2 cups heavy (or whipping) cream
2 teaspoons drained whole green peppercorns packed in brine
2 tablespoons imported coarse-grained Dijon mustard
2 tablespoons imported smooth Dijon mustard
Sea or coarse salt and freshly ground black pepper to taste

1. Place the skillet that the Salt-Crusted Beef Tenderloin was seared in back on a burner over medium-high heat. Add the shallots and sauté until they just begin to brown, 2 to 3 minutes. Add

the Cognac to the pan and continue cooking until it has reduced by half, 4 to 5 minutes.

2. Add the heavy cream to the skillet and stir in the green peppercorns. Continue reducing the sauce over medium heat until it is reduced by half again, about 10 minutes. Keep the sauce warm over very low heat, and as close to serving time as possible, swirl in the mustards until thoroughly blended. Season the sauce with salt and pepper. Serve warm.

MAKES ABOUT 1½ CUPS

TOMATO-MUSTARD COULIS

This summery sauce is a somewhat more healthful accompaniment to the Salt-Crusted Beef Tenderloin than the Creamy Cognac and Mustard Sauce.

6 plum tomatoes, seeded and diced
3 shallots, minced
3 cloves garlic, minced
3 tablespoons fresh tarragon, minced
¼ cup imported coarse-grained Dijon mustard
1 cup Homemade Beef Stock (page 27)
1 large egg
½ cup olive oil
Sea or coarse salt and freshly ground black pepper
*   to taste*

1. Combine the tomatoes, shallots, garlic, tarragon, mustard, and stock in a medium-size saucepan and bring to a boil over medium-high heat. Simmer for 5 minutes, stirring occasionally.

2. Pour the hot tomato mixture into a food processor and process until fairly smooth. Add the egg while the mixture is still hot and process until incorporated. With the machine running, pour the olive oil through the feed tube in a thin and steady stream. Season the mixture to taste with salt and pepper. Use at once or keep warm on top of a double boiler set over barely simmering water.

MAKES ABOUT 2½ CUPS

151

Boeuf Beaujolaise

Onomatopoetically, I believe *Beaujolais* to be just about the happiest-sounding word in the world. As a region, it is also one of the most delightful for cycling. The vineyards of Gamay grapes are tiered over rounded hillsides interspersed with quaint stone hamlets and forests fragrant with pine and chestnut. The biking itself may be more challenging with the roller-coaster pops up and down hills, but it's likely to feel painless because the temptation to stop and taste the fruity and floral wines of the land is everywhere. In Burgundy, no place better exemplifies the unique coexistence of the sensual with the spiritual than the village of Julienas's wine-tasting *caveau* housed in the town's old church— a watering hole sacred to many of my cyclists. No wonder any recipe made with Beaujolais wine seems blessed!

Here, rosy steaks are napped with a coarse but flavorful Beaujolais-based sauce that has been studded liberally with minced shallots, celery, carrots, garlic, and green peppercorns. The pan-seared steaks are served sliced rather than whole so that the sauce literally seeps into all the surfaces of the meat. The Potato Gratin Dijonnaise (page 87) makes a perfect accompaniment. Guests' spirits will of course become one with the wine if plenty of extra bottles of Beaujolais are kept flowing.

152

3 tablespoons dry mustard

1½ tablespoons coarsely cracked black pepper

2 teaspoons sea salt, plus additional to taste

6 boneless shell, strip, or sirloin steaks (10 to 12 ounces each),
     at least 1 inch thick

6 tablespoons (¾ stick) unsalted butter

2 tablespoons olive or vegetable oil

4 shallots, minced

1 rib celery, minced

1 carrot, peeled and minced

2 teaspoons dried tarragon

2 whole bay leaves

1½ tablespoons drained coarsely cracked green peppercorns

2½ cups red Beaujolais wine

3 cloves garlic, minced

2 tablespoons marc de Bourgogne or brandy

½ cup minced fresh parsley

1. Preheat the oven to 325°F.

2. In a small bowl, stir together the dry mustard, black pepper, and 2 teaspoons salt. Rub this mixture lightly into both sides of the steaks to season them.

3. Heat 1 tablespoon of the butter with the oil in a very large skillet over medium-high heat. Add the steaks to the skillet and sauté 4 to 5 minutes per side for rare to medium-rare meat. Transfer the steaks to a platter, cover loosely with aluminum foil, and keep warm in the oven while making the sauce. (The steaks will continue to cook a bit, so keep this in mind when deciding how long to cook them.)

4. Add the shallots, celery, carrot, tarragon, bay leaves, and green peppercorns to the skillet and sauté over medium-high heat for 2 minutes. Add the wine and boil until the liquid is reduced by half, 10 to 12 minutes. Discard the bay leaves, and stir in the garlic and *marc de Bourgogne* or brandy. Reduce the heat to low and stir in the remaining 5 tablespoons butter, tablespoon by tablespoon, to make a lightly emulsified sauce. Season with salt and stir in the parsley.

5. Slice the steaks ½ inch thick and fan them out onto dinner plates. Nap generously with the Beaujolais sauce and serve at once.

MAKES 6 SERVINGS

THE TERROIR'S THE THING

Good wine makers in Burgundy strive to respect the history and God-given conditions of the plots of earth where they grow grapes. Herein lies the notion of *terroir,* defined by Al Hotchkin of the beloved Burgundy Wine Company in New York City: "Not only the soil, but the slope, the drainage, the microclimate; that is, all the factors affecting a particular plot of ground. Perhaps the word *environment* comes the closest to expressing the concept of *terroir.*"

Matt Kramer, in his wonderful book *Making Sense of Burgundy,* explains the more mystical element of *terroir:* "But *terroir* holds yet another dimension: It sanctions what cannot be measured, yet still located and savored. *Terroir* prospects for differences. In this it is at odds with science, which demands proof by replication rather than in a shining uniqueness."

In trying to distill the notion of *terroir* for this book, I attended an in-depth seminar in New York run by Al Hotchkin. The subject was presented as "*Terroir*—Does it exist?—If so, what is it?—Or is it 'all just dirt' and the wine maker that count?" After a few heavenly hours of tasting, I was amazed by my knack for detecting the *goût de terroir*—taste that is unique to the wine from a specific vineyard—when blind-tasting samples. Since I don't attend a lot of fancy wine tastings, I surmised that much of my nose for Burgundy wines must have developed from years of cycling through Burgundy vineyards. Indeed, if you are a sensitive cyclist, you smell, see, feel, and often taste (!) the subtle differences and nuances between vineyards as you pedal along. Now I fully understand why the Burgundians tending to the *terroir* in their individual vineyards greet us cyclists with such warmth and enthusiasm. And twenty years of sipping while cycling in Burgundy has made me one confirmed *terroirist.*

154

Grilled Lamb Chops la Côte d'Or

Bernard Loiseau's La Côte d'Or restaurant in Saulieu is one of Burgundy's more controversial Michelin-starred restaurants. The Gault-Millau reviewing team named it "Restaurant of 1986," but many find Loiseau's calorie-lightened cuisine disappointing in the context of a supposed gastronomic temple. Predictably, I have here gravitated toward one of La Côte d'Or's richer and more buttery recipes—*selle d'agneau au beurre de noix*—roasted saddle of lamb in an unusual and absolutely delectable toasted walnut sauce. For home cooking, I have made the recipe more rustic and accessible by substituting shoulder lamb chops or bone-in center-cut lamb steaks for the saddle and by restyling the sauce slightly. The resulting flavors are still sensational. I suggest pouring a lesser-known appellation from the Côte de Beaune, such as a red Monthelie or Santenay, as an amiable quaff.

155

2 cups Homemade Beef Stock (page 27)
½ cup walnut halves
2 cloves garlic, minced
2 tablespoons minced fresh tarragon, or 2 teaspoons dried
8 tablespoons (1 stick) unsalted butter, at room temperature
2 teaspoons honey
Sea or coarse salt and freshly ground black pepper to taste
4 shoulder lamb chops or 4 bone-in center-cut lamb steaks
    (8 to 10 ounces each)
2 tablespoons olive oil

1. Preheat a toaster oven or regular oven to 400°F.

2. Place the beef stock in a medium-size saucepan, bring to a boil, and simmer until reduced by half, 7 to 10 minutes. Keep the reduced stock warm over very low heat. Meanwhile, bring 2 cups of water to a boil in another saucepan. Add the walnuts and blanch for 30 seconds; drain immediately and dry with paper towels. Spread the nuts on a small baking sheet and bake until lightly browned, 5 to 7 minutes. Let them cool completely.

3. Prepare a fire for grilling, or if cooking indoors, preheat the broiler.

4. Place the walnuts, garlic, and tarragon in a food processor and process until finely minced. Add the butter and continue processing until smooth. Whisk the walnut butter, tablespoon by table-spoon, into the warm, reduced beef stock. Take care not to let the heat get too high or the sauce will  break. When all the butter has been incorporated, whisk in the honey and adjust the seasoning with salt and pepper to taste. Keep the sauce warm over very low heat while cooking the lamb.

5. Brush the lamb lightly all over with the oil and season on both sides with salt and pepper. Grill or broil the lamb 5 inches away from the heat, turning once, until cooked to desired degree of doneness, 7 to 8 minutes for rare to medium-rare meat. Pool the walnut sauce over the bottom of each serving plate and top with the lamb. Serve at once.

MAKES 4 SERVINGS

PINOT ENVY

Pinot envy—a blind passion for red Burgundies and all other wines of rumored resemblance—is one affliction I am elated to have. Not only do I pass rapturous hours bicycling through Burgundy's patchwork vineyards, I brake for them, part with irrational sums of money for coveted bottles that can disappoint as readily as dazzle, and spend mealtimes dreaming about elusive yet existent pinot noir perfection. I've been known to say unkind things about cabernet sauvignon and form instant friendships with those who also share an impassioned penchant for pinot noir. It's no wonder that I took Marq de Villiers's hot-off-the-press book, *The Heartbreak Grape*, about how vintner Josh Jensen of the Calera Wine Company managed to produce superb pinot noir in California, to bed with me for three nights straight. The passage from this book that follows is cited as further illumination of pinot envy:

> When it comes right down to it, all winemaking is similar— it's the process of helping grapes ferment themselves into wine.
>
> But, clearly, some methods of encouraging this process are better than others.
>
> The Pinot Noir is one of the more difficult ones.
>
> In those innocent days when gender descriptives were still thought amusing, the Pinot Noir was called feminine—by which was meant flighty, changeable, beguiling and seductive.
>
> In the same vein, they called it the heartbreak grape because it was so stubborn, so particular, so elusive, so damn difficult to get right. And also because when it was at its best it made the most sublime wine of all. The heartbreak grape? You can't break a heart without having captured it first.

Venison Ragoût with Whole Cloves of Garlic and Dried Fruits

∽

F rance has an awesome system of well-marked and maintained small departmental roads that crisscross its lush countryside. These rural roads are a godsend for cyclists, as we can often bike for miles on them without having our sense of oneness with our spectacular surroundings marred by passing cars. The roads are also conducive to biking abreast in pairs, so that the most picturesque moments are often shared with a fellow bikemate from the tour I am leading.

In my mind, cycling in pairs in Burgundy takes on special significance because much of the daily chatter with the local *vignerons* we meet revolves around the *pairing* of their wines with specific Burgundian dishes. Soon, I find myself unable to resist thinking about the new bonds of friendship I witness forming among biking companions in terms pertinent to the locale. So it is that the single lady from California seems to synchronize with the lawyer from Toronto like Chablis and oysters. Or, that the two couples from Texas begin to stick together like *Cru* Beaujolais wines from neighboring vineyards.

Back home without vineyard expanses and group intrigue to feed my pairing palate, I often turn to my brother Jonathan for trustworthy food and wine matchmaking advice. Jonathan runs a bistro-style restaurant with an award-winning wine list along the coast of Maine and often hosts wine-tasting dinners during the blustery winter months. Raving about venison's affinity for red Burgundy wines, he offered to share this hearty stew recipe, wherein the venison meat is simmered in a delicious combination of lots of garlic, beer, dried cherries, apricots, and prunes.

The recipe is by no means a typical Burgundy combination but all the fruits marvelously pick up the fruity undertones found in many a red Burgundy wine. Try pairing the ragoût with a robust red Pommard from just south of Beaune or a fruity Beaujolais, such as a Fleurie or Juliènas.

1¼ cups unbleached all-purpose flour
Sea or coarse salt and freshly ground black pepper
    to taste
3 pounds venison stew meat (from the shoulder or loin),
    cut into 1½-inch cubes
5 tablespoons olive or vegetable oil
1 large onion, minced
30 cloves garlic, peeled
1½ bottles (12 ounces each) of your favorite lager
    or ale
2 teaspoons dried thyme
⅔ cup dried cherries
½ cup pitted prunes
½ cup dried apricot halves

159

1. Preheat the oven to 325°F.

2. Mix the flour with a generous sprinkling of salt and pepper, and then dredge the venison in the seasoned flour, shaking off any excess. Heat the oil over medium heat in a Dutch oven or other ovenproof casserole. Brown the venison cubes in batches until lightly browned on all sides, about 5 minutes per batch. Transfer each batch to a platter or shallow bowl as it is browned.

3. Add the onions to the pot and sauté until softened, about 5 minutes. Add the garlic cloves and beer and stir to scrape up any browned bits that may be stuck to the bottom of the pot. Add the thyme and then return the venison to the pot and mix in the cherries, prunes, and apricots. Adjust the seasoning with salt and pepper, if necessary.

4. Cover the ragoût tightly with a lid or aluminum foil. Bake until the meat is tender and the vegetables and fruits have begun to disintegrate and thicken the ragout, 2 to 2½ hours. Serve hot.

MAKES 6 SERVINGS

JUST DESSERTS

Bûche de Bourgogne

Cassis Crisp

Chocolate Boule

This chapter offers a plausible explanation of why Burgundians grow to resemble their wine barrels and why cyclists, exercise notwithstanding, soon find themselves growing to resemble Burgundians. Candy may be dandy and liquor quicker, but in Burgundy, liqueur-laced candies and sweets are deemed the most irresistible of all. A warm chocolate *boule* arrives as chef-prescribed medicine for polishing off those last sips of artery-cleansing red Burgundy, while proper manners dictate that Le Montrachet's Apple Tart be eaten in its entirety while still piping hot. And there's no better for jet-lag-induced insomnia than a nightcap, *marc*-fortified (decaffeinated!) Café Chez Camille.

In a region so rich in gastronomy, one should, of course, expect a dazzling array of "just" desserts.

Bûche de Bourgogne

This rolled cake naturally takes its inspiration from the famous French yule-log cake served at Christmas, but my version is restyled to feature an intriguing juxtaposition of Burgundy-beloved earthy chestnuts with silky *marc*-fortified chocolate.

CHOCOLATE HAZELNUT SPONGE CAKE

4 large eggs
⅓ cup (packed) light brown sugar
1 teaspoon vanilla extract
Pinch of salt
⅓ cup granulated sugar
1 cup lightly toasted hazelnuts, skinned and finely ground
⅓ cup unbleached all-purpose flour
3 tablespoons unsweetened cocoa powder
4 tablespoons (½ stick) unsalted butter, melted and cooled,
    plus extra (unmelted) for buttering pan

CHESTNUT BUTTERCREAM

½ cup granulated sugar
3 tablespoons water
4 large egg yolks
¾ cup (1½ sticks) unsalted butter, at room temperature
1 cup unsweetened chestnut purée (available tinned in specialty
    food stores)
1½ tablespoons marc de Bourgogne or brandy
Confectioners' sugar for dusting

CHOCOLATE ICING AND FINISHING

⅔ cup granulated sugar
1 tablespoon instant coffee granules
½ cup heavy (or whipping) cream
3 ounces unsweetened chocolate, finely chopped
4 tablespoons (½ stick) unsalted butter, at room temperature
1½ tablespoons marc de Bourgogne or brandy
10 whole candied chestnuts in syrup (available in specialty
    food stores)
Confectioners' sugar for sprinkling

1. To make the sponge cake, preheat the oven to 350°F. Butter a 15 x 10-inch jelly-roll pan, then line it with a piece of parchment paper cut ½ inch smaller than the pan. Butter the paper.

2. Separate 3 of the eggs, placing the yolks in a large bowl and the whites in a medium-size one. Add the remaining whole egg to the yolks and whisk until blended. Using an electric mixer, slowly beat in the brown sugar and vanilla. Continue beating at high speed until the mixture is very light, about 3 minutes.

3. Using clean beaters, beat the egg whites until they just begin to hold their shape. Beat in the salt and then gradually beat in the granulated sugar. Continue beating until the whites are very glossy and hold firm peaks.

164

4. Using a rubber spatula, gently fold the whites into the yolk mixture. Sprinkle the ground nuts over the batter and gently fold them in. Sift the flour and cocoa together over the batter and carefully fold them in until the batter is smooth. Take care not to overmix the batter. Finally, fold in the melted butter.

5. Spread the batter into the prepared pan in a smooth and even layer. Bake until a toothpick inserted in the middle of the cake comes out clean, 15 to 17 minutes.

6. Using a sharp knife, trim ¼ inch of cake from all sides. Invert the cake onto a clean kitchen towel dusted lightly with confectioners' sugar. Peel away the parchment paper and, starting with a long side, roll up the cake in the towel like a jelly roll. Let it cool completely on a wire rack.

7. Prepare the chestnut buttercream: Combine the sugar and water in a small saucepan and bring to a boil over medium heat.

Continue cooking until the mixture reaches 245°F on a candy thermometer, 4 to 5 minutes.

8. Meanwhile, beat the egg yolks until thickened and light in a medium-size, heat-proof bowl, about 2 minutes. Pour the hot sugar syrup in a thin steady stream into the yolks while you continue beating the yolks. Continue beating for several minutes until the mixture is thick, has tripled in volume, and has cooled to room temperature. Beat in the butter, tablespoon by tablespoon, to make a smooth and spreadable buttercream. Then beat in the chestnut purée and the *marc de Bourgogne.*

9. Unroll the sponge cake and spread the top evenly with the buttercream. Reroll the cake and place it on a long serving plate. Store in the refrigerator while making the chocolate icing.

10. To make the icing: Combine the sugar, coffee granules, and cream in a small saucepan. Bring to a boil over medium heat, stirring constantly. Reduce the heat to low and simmer 5 minutes without stirring. Remove from the heat, add the chocolate, and stir until melted. Whisk in the butter and the *marc* to make a smooth mixture. Refrigerate the icing for several minutes to thicken it to spreading consistency, but do not allow it to become firm.

165

11. To finish the *bûche,* cut a diagonal slice about 3 inches wide, from one end of the cake roll. Place the slice about one-third of the way down the roll to resemble a branch on a log. Spread the top and sides of the cake with the chocolate icing. Decorate the cake, either on the top or along the sides, with the candied chestnuts. Store the cake in the refrigerator until ready to serve. Cut the cake into 1-inch slices and garnish each serving with a whole chestnut. Dust around the sides of the cake with sifted confectioners' sugar for the look of freshly fallen snow. Serve—and relish a reward for all your efforts.

MAKES 8 TO 10 SERVINGS

MADAME MASSON AND HER CHÂTEAU DE GEVREY-CHAMBERTIN

Wine tours and tastings abound throughout the Côte d'Or, but one of the most unusual and memorable ones is conducted by Madame Masson at her imposing château on the fringes of the village of Gevrey-Chambertin. I can remember touring with Madame Masson back in my teens. She is now well into her eighties and still going strong. The Masson family had achieved and sustained nobility by lending money to Louis XIII and then managing to escape the guillotine during the French Revolution. Madame Masson, however, wouldn't mind seeing a return to the old ways and feudalism.

Highlights of the château tour include entering the *grande salle,* where in order to preserve the floor for a few hundred years more, everyone is asked to remove their shoes and slide across the room on pairs of worn pot holders. Guests are also forewarned never to mention the word *toilette* in Madame's presence, since Madame's own, off-limits WC is the only one in the entire château. Winemaking methods at the château are yet another curiosity, for they are not only organic but incredibly antiquated.

The property's *Grand Cru* Charmes, *Premier Cru,* and Château Gevrey-Chambertin are all decent but by no means fabulous. Still, it's hard to resist buying a few bottles, since Madame Masson personally glues on the labels and seals the tops with wax that she keeps on her back burner like a pot of witch's brew. The years etched onto the wine labels will often be chosen for tax purposes rather than vintage. Open a bottle of Madame Masson's Gevrey-Chambertin and you are drinking history, not all those other snobbish elements that wine connoisseurs have brainwashed us to identify in Côte de Nuits wines.

Warm Chocolate Boules with Strawberry-Beaujolais Sauce

Pardon the pun, but the craze for sinfully rich, warm chocolate cakes and tarts with molten interiors has of late oozed from France to North America. While I'm not much of a fan of elaborate desserts, or of chocolate, I must confess to a weakness for these, particularly in the context of Burgundian dining. There is nothing better than ending a Burgundian feast with an elegant chocolate finale, an incentive for polishing off the last sips of a great bottle of Côtes de Nuits red. Chocolate and pinot noir may be flavors that spring from the earth, but the combination of the two must surely be heaven-sent.

In the home kitchen, the individual chocolate *boules* are easily baked in everyday muffin tins. The runny centers are achieved by inserting homemade truffles into each cake's center before baking. All can be assembled in advance and then popped into the oven toward the end of dinner to ensure a meltingly momentous presentation. The Strawberry-Beaujolais Sauce is inspired

by Mark Peel and Nancy Silverton's *At Home* cookbook. I also enjoy serving these chocolate *boules* surrounded by *crème anglaise* or topped with a scoop of coffee ice cream.

STRAWBERRY-BEAUJOLAIS SAUCE
⅔ *cup sugar*
¼ *cup water*
10 *whole black peppercorns*
½ *vanilla bean, split lengthwise*
4 *whole cloves*
1 *cinnamon stick (3 inches)*
1 *bottle (750 ml) Beaujolais wine*
2 *quarts strawberries, hulled and halved*

WARM CHOCOLATE BOULES
11 *tablespoons unsalted butter*
9 *ounces best-quality bittersweet chocolate
      (I like Callebaut)·*
3 *tablespoons heavy (or whipping) cream*
2 *tablespoons favorite after-dinner liqueur, such as
      Grand Marnier, Chambord, Frangelico, or Cognac*
3 *large eggs plus 3 large egg yolks*
½ *cup sugar*
½ *cup unbleached all-purpose flour*

1. Make the Strawberry-Beaujolais Sauce: In a large, heavy saucepan, combine the sugar, water, peppercorns, vanilla bean, cloves, and cinnamon stick. Bring to a boil and cook until the liquid turns a golden caramel color, 5 to 6 minutes. Remove from the heat, and taking care to stand back, slowly pour in the bottle of Beaujolais. The wine will spatter initially as it hits the hot syrup, and then the syrup will begin to harden. Return the saucepan to the burner and

cook over medium-high heat, stirring well to remelt the caramel. Let the liquid boil gently until it has reduced by half, 20 to 25 minutes. Strain into another large, clean saucepan and discard the spices.

2. Add the strawberries to the wine syrup, bring the mixture back to a boil, and cook for 2 minutes. Remove from heat and let cool to room temperature. (The sauce may stand for up to 5 hours before using.)

3. To make the chocolate *boules,* melt 1 tablespoon of the butter and brush it lightly over the 12 cups of a standard muffin tin. Set aside.

4. To make the truffles for the cakes' centers, break 4 ounces of the chocolate into small pieces and combine with the cream in a small, heavy saucepan. Melt over low heat, stirring constantly, until absolutely smooth. Remove from the heat and stir in the liqueur. Transfer the chocolate mixture to a small dish, place in the freezer, and chill until the chocolate firms but is still malleable enough to shape into a ball, 20 to 30 minutes.

5. To make the chocolate *boules* batter, break the remaining 5 ounces chocolate into small pieces and combine with the remaining 10 tablespoons butter in a medium-size heavy saucepan. Melt over low heat, stirring constantly, until smooth. Remove from the heat. In a large mixing bowl, beat the eggs, egg yolks, and sugar together until the mixture thickens and triples in volume, 7 to 8 minutes. Fold in the melted chocolate mixture. Sift the flour over the batter and then quickly fold it in.

6. Spoon the batter into the prepared muffin cups, filling each about two-thirds full. Using a melon baller or rounded teaspoon, scoop twelve 1-inch-round balls from the truffle mixture. Push each ball down into the center of each cake. The *boules* may be made up to this point and held for several hours before baking. If holding for more than an hour or two, store in the refrigerator until ready to bake.

169

7. When ready to bake, preheat the oven to 350°F.

8. Bake the *boules* in the middle of the oven until the tops spring back when touched lightly, 12 to 13 minutes. Remove from the oven and let them cool for 2 to 3 minutes. Run a knife gently around the edges of each *boule,* and then invert the entire tin onto a flat baking sheet. Using a spatula, transfer the *boules* to serving plates. Surround generously with the strawberry Beaujolais sauce and serve at once.

MAKES 12 SERVINGS

Vine Leaf Cookies

After confirming that I could successfully make Lameloise's Pinot Noir *Granité* (page 183) at home and then enjoying it on several occasions scooped into wine goblets for dessert, I started to hanker for an interesting cookie accompaniment. Out of the blue, or perhaps I should say "the Burgundy," the notion of making these cookies in the shape of vine leaves struck me. Now, a cookie cutter in the shape of a vine leaf isn't the easiest gadget to come by, and some of my attempts at free-form leaves left some realism to be desired, but I still insist the idea is too "di-vine" to give up on. I know there are maple leaf cookie cutters to be had in New England and Canada, and cookies made from these could always be styled to look more like vine leaves. And there's also the chance that someone might thrill me by starting to make cookie cutters in the shape of a vine leaf. And of course, there are myriad other shapes into which to cut these cookies. Aesthetics aside, the combination of the lemon and anise scent of the cookies and the winy *granité* is not to be missed.

2½ cups unbleached all-purpose flour
½ cup plus 3 tablespoons sugar
Pinch of salt
8 tablespoons (1 stick) chilled unsalted butter, cut
    into small pieces
4 ounces chilled cream cheese, cut into small
    pieces
Finely grated zest of 1 lemon
1½ teaspoons anise seeds
3 tablespoons chilled dry white wine
2 large egg whites beaten with 2 tablespoons water

171

1. Place the flour, the ½ cup sugar, salt, butter, cream cheese, lemon zest, and anise seeds in a food processor. Process until the mixture resembles coarse meal. Add the wine and process until the mixture begins to form a ball. Shape the dough into a flat disk, wrap in plastic wrap, and refrigerate for at least 1 hour.

2. Preheat the oven to 350°F. Line baking sheets with parchment paper.

3. Divide the dough in half. Place one half on a lightly floured surface and the other in the refrigerator. Roll the dough to a thickness of ¼ inch. Using a leaf-shaped cookie cutter (or another shape), cut out the cookies and arrange 1 inch apart on the baking sheets. If making leaves, use the point of a small, sharp knife to engrave veins into each leaf. Repeat the process until all the dough (including the half in the refrigerator) and scraps have been used.

4. Glaze the cookies by brushing them lightly all over with the beaten egg whites and water. Sprinkle the tops lightly with the

remaining 3 tablespoons sugar. Bake the cookies until just beginning to color, 10 to 12 minutes. Transfer to a wire rack to cool.
Because of the pastrylike nature of these cookies, they are best if
consumed within 24 hours of baking. The cookies may also be frozen
after baking to preserve their freshness.

MAKES 24 TO 30 COOKIES

Warm Apple Tarts
Le Montrachet

172

One of the bicycle trips I guided in Burgundy began with a
few nights at the warm and friendly Hôtel le Montrachet,
in the little village of Puligny-Montrachet. Although we stay in
grander hotels as the trip progresses, the people in my group
(myself included) simply adored the easy ambience of this hotel.
It is, after all, tough to beat a location that affords a warm-up
jaunt through the world's most famous white wine vineyards followed by an evening stroll to a private wine tasting with the
charming and legendary Olivier Leflaive, at his home, a mere two
doors down from the hotel.

We dined both nights at Le Montrachet's fine restaurant, and
the warm apple tart we were treated to our first night lingered
on in everyone's memory. The hotel's hosts, Thierry and Suzanne
Gazagnes, couldn't have been kinder about sharing the recipe.
They invited me into the kitchen one early morning so I could
watch it being made firsthand and then insisted I enjoy the sam-

ple tart while ensconced in a cozy nook in the hotel's friendly bar.

The tart requires a few advance preparations, but it really isn't very difficult to make. Since the pleasure of eating this tart lies in its hot and puffy splendor as it emerges from the oven, I assemble my tarts in advance, store them in the refrigerator, and then bake them as my guests and I are enjoying dinner. At Le Montrachet, the apple tart is served with a cupped *tuile*, or thin cookie, holding a scoop of apple sorbet; at home, however, I'm quite content to let my tarts have all the glory and thus eliminate the sorbet.

CANDIED ORANGE ZEST
1 large orange
¾ cup granulated sugar
1 cup water

SUGAR SYRUP
¾ cup granulated sugar
⅓ cup water
2 tablespoons Calvados or brandy

TARTS
1 package (17¼ ounces) frozen puff pastry,
*   thawed*
4 or 5 Granny Smith apples
2 tablespoons unsalted butter, melted
⅓ cup granulated sugar
Sifted confectioners' sugar, for garnishing

1. Make the candied orange zest: Using a vegetable peeler, remove the zest from the orange in large strips. With a sharp knife, cut the strips into a fine julienne. Fill a small saucepan with water, bring to

173

a boil, and blanch the zest for 2 minutes; drain thoroughly.

2. Cook ½ cup of the sugar with the cup of water in a small heavy saucepan over medium heat, stirring to dissolve the sugar. Increase the heat to a boil and add the zest. Reduce to a simmer and cook for 15 minutes. Using a slotted spoon, remove the zest from the saucepan and drain on a plate. When cool, toss the zest with the remaining ¼ cup sugar to coat evenly. Separate the zest into individual strips and store in an airtight container for up to 1 week.

3. Make the sugar syrup: Combine the sugar and water in a small heavy saucepan and cook over medium heat, stirring to dissolve the sugar completely, 4 to 5 minutes. Remove from heat and stir in the Calvados. The syrup may be stored in a jar in the refrigerator indefinitely.

4. When ready to assemble the tarts, preheat the oven to 450°F. Line two large baking sheets with parchment paper.

5. Separate the 2 sheets of puff pastry and roll each out on a lightly floured surface to increase the size by about half. Trace and cut out three 7-inch circles from each sheet of puff pastry. (Save the scraps for another use or discard them.) Arrange 3 circles on each baking sheet.

6. Peel and core the apples. Slice very thin. Scatter 5 or 6 pieces of the candied orange zest over each puff pastry circle. Arrange the apples so that the slices overlap slightly in concentric rings to cover each circle. Brush the apples lightly with the melted butter and then sprinkle lightly all over with the granulated sugar. If not baking the tarts immediately, store them in the refrigerator until ready to bake.

7. Bake the tarts until puffed and golden brown, 17 to 20 minutes. Remove from the oven and immediately drizzle each with 2 tablespoons of the sugar syrup. Transfer the tarts to serving plates, dust all over with the sifted confectioners' sugar, and serve at once.

MAKES 6 INDIVIDUAL TARTS

THE HORIZON OF THE PEASANT GROWERS extends as far as the next village; their traditions and habits are rooted in the immediate locality. But they cultivate vines which produce each year such precious grapes that millionaires in London and Tokyo, Paris and New York, vie with one another to secure a tiny allocation of the treasured product. Such consumers, unconcerned to probe beneath the shuttered surface of village life, unwilling to stretch their legs by a walk through the vineyards, miss out on one of the greatest pleasures of wine, its testimony of the place. The taste changes at every moment and is summarized in the sense of smell, so elusive and immediate, which provides us with sudden jumps of memory, recalling the past with greater urgency than any other stimulus. And the scent of those fabulous white Burgundies (a mixture of fresh straw and ripe peaches, an earthy intensity underlying the elegance, suggestions of woodsmoke, of honey and of freshly sawn oak) will always be a summary to me of a quite particular locality, evoking more swiftly and completely than any other record a small village in Burgundy with a seductive name: Puligny-Montrachet.

—SIMON LOFTUS
PULIGNY-MONTRACHET—
JOURNAL OF A VILLAGE IN BURGUNDY

175

Colette's Lemon Tart

∾

Ⅰf you are lucky enough to have both traveled at a leisurely pace about the backroads of Burgundy and relished the novels of the sensualist supreme, Colette, then it should come as no surprise that this greatly admired French female writer was born of lusty Burgundy soil. I have yet to determine whether I'm more inspired by Colette's well-crafted musings on love or those on gastronomy . . . or the two as they commingle . . . but who can forget her wonderful piece of advice in *Prisons et paradis:* "If I had a son of marriageable age, I should say to him: 'Beware of young women who love neither wine nor truffles nor cheese nor music.'" I do, however, know I am unequivocal in my passion for her lemon tart.

I happened upon what is believed to be Colette's original recipe while reading a book (*In Search of the Perfect Meal*) by another author whose work I enjoy, Roy Andries de Groot. As it turns out, de Groot was also a great fan of Colette's and liked to imagine her eating her favorite dessert described by him as "a freshly baked, still-warm-from-the-oven, soft, tangy, and velvety *tarte au citron,* a lemon tart of buttery-creamy-rich taste and texture," in the sunlit pink bedroom on the huge brass bed with the young twenty-three-year-old lover depicted in her novel *Cheri.*

Since I, too, have a lovely pink bedroom and a fine imagination (but unfortunately neither a big brass bed nor my own private twenty-three-year-old Adonis), I set immediately to fashioning the following surrogate version of Colette's sublime tart.

Here is a close approximation of the recipe as de Groot recorded it in an essay entitled "From One Who Loved Food As Much As Sex: An Easy Lemon Pie."

PASTRY SHELL

1⅓ cups unbleached all-purpose flour

8 tablespoons (1 stick) chilled unsalted butter, cut into small pieces

Pinch of salt

1 egg yolk, slightly beaten

2 to 2½ tablespoons chilled orange flower water (available at some specialty food stores)

LEMON FILLING

4 extra-large eggs

⅔ cup sugar

2 large lemons, zest peeled and finely minced, juice squeezed and reserved

1 tablespoon cornstarch

177

1. To make the pastry shell, place the flour, butter, and salt in a food processor and process to cut the butter evenly into the flour. Add the egg yolk and with the machine running, pour enough of the chilled orange flower water through the feed tube so that the dough just begins to stick together. (Take care not to overprocess the dough.) Using your hands, gather the pastry together, form into a flat disk, wrap in plastic wrap, and refrigerate for at least 1 hour.

2. Preheat the oven to 375°F.

3. On a lightly floured surface, roll out the pastry into a 13-inch circle. Carefully transfer the pastry to a 10-inch fluted tart pan with a removable bottom. Trim and crimp the edges of the pastry and prick the bottom lightly all over with the tines of a fork. Line the shell with aluminum foil and then weigh it down with either

metal pie weights or dried beans.

4. Bake the pastry shell until just set and beginning to color slightly, about 15 minutes. Remove the foil and weights and let the shell cool while making the filling. Leave the oven set at 375°F.

5. To make the filling, separate the egg yolks and whites, placing the yolks in the top of a double boiler, off the heat, and the whites in a smaller medium-size mixing bowl (copper if you have it). With a hand-held electric mixer, beat ⅓ cup of the sugar into the egg yolks and continue beating until the mixture becomes a light and creamy pale yellow, about 5 minutes more. Beat in the lemon zest, juice, and cornstarch until smooth and incorporated. While you are beating the egg yolks, bring some water to a simmer in the bottom of the double boiler.

6. Set the egg yolk mixture in the top of the double boiler over the simmering water. Stir it constantly with a wooden spoon until it thickens to a custard, usually 7 to 10 minutes. Remove from the heat and continue to stir constantly for 2 or 3 minutes more as the mixture cools.

7. With clean beaters, beat the egg whites until frothy and then gradually beat in, tablespoon by tablespoon, the remaining ⅓ cup sugar. Continue to beat until the egg whites form stiff and shiny peaks. Gently but thoroughly fold the egg whites into the warm lemon custard, as if you were making a soufflé. Spread the filling evenly over the prebaked tart shell, smoothing the top lightly with a rubber spatula.

8. Bake the tart in the center of the oven until the filling is puffed up, lightly browned, and set, 25 to 30 minutes. Let the tart cool (the filling will sink as it cools) for at least 15 minutes before cutting into wedges and serving warm. Alternatively, the tart can be baked in advance, cooled, and reheated for 10 minutes in a 325°F oven before serving.

MAKES 8 SERVINGS

Raspberry and Cassis Bavarian Cream

∽

T his is definitely the dessert for those who get their kicks from cassis! It's also a great finale for cooks who love the ease of being able to make a very pretty and sophisticated dessert ahead of time.

LEMON- AND VANILLA-SCENTED LADYFINGER CAKE
Butter and flour for preparing the pan
3 large eggs, separated
½ cup sugar
1 teaspoon vanilla extract
2 teaspoons grated lemon zest
⅔ cup unbleached all-purpose flour

BAVARIAN CREAM
1 bag (12 ounces) frozen whole
*   unsweetened raspberries,*
*   partially defrosted*
1 tablespoon sugar
⅛ cup cassis
1 envelope unflavored gelatin
2 cups heavy (or whipping) cream

GARNISHES
⅔ cup cassis
Fresh raspberries

179

1. Preheat the oven to 325°F. Lightly butter and flour a 15 x 10-inch jelly-roll pan.

2. To make the ladyfinger cake, use an electric mixer to beat the egg yolks and 2 tablespoons of the sugar together in a medium-size bowl until thick and light colored, 3 to 4 minutes. Beat in the vanilla extract and lemon zest. In a separate bowl, and using clean beaters, beat the egg whites until soft peaks form. Continue beating, gradually adding the remaining ¼ cup plus 2 tablespoons sugar, until stiff peaks form.

3. Using a rubber spatula, gently fold one-third of the egg whites into the yolk mixture. Once they are incorporated, gently fold in the remaining two-thirds of the whites. Sift one-third of the flour over the egg mixture and then gently fold it in. Repeat the process with the remaining flour. Spread the batter evenly into the prepared pan. Bake in the center of the oven until the cake is firm and turns light golden, about 15 minutes. Cool completely in the pan.

180

4. To make the Bavarian cream, purée the raspberries and sugar together in a food processor. Strain the purée through a sieve to remove the seeds. Combine the purée and the cassis in a medium-size saucepan. Sprinkle the envelope of gelatin over the top. Warm the mixture over low heat, stirring to dissolve the gelatin, 3 to 4 minutes. Let cool to room temperature.

5. Meanwhile, lightly butter eight 1½-cup soufflé dishes or ramekins. Cut 8 circles the same size as the molds from the ladyfinger cake. (Save the scraps from the cake for nibbling or some other creative use.) Line the bottom of each mold with a cake round.

6. Beat the cream in a chilled bowl until fairly stiff peaks form. Pour in the cooled raspberry-cassis mixture and continue beating until thoroughly incorporated. Spoon the Bavarian cream into the molds and then chill until the cream has set, at least 3 hours.

7. When ready to serve, run a knife around the insides of the molds and unmold onto serving plates. Invert so that the cake sides are down. Drizzle some cassis over and around each Bavarian cream. Garnish with a few fresh raspberries and serve.

MAKES 8 INDIVIDUAL DESSERTS

181

Cassis Crisp

As a guide, I always do as I encourage my cyclists to do and therefore never leave Burgundy without a good supply of Domaine Lucien Jacob's fabulous cassis in protective tow. After sipping a surfeit of kirs, my thoughts inevitably turn to creative cassis cookery with cues frequently directed by the flavors professional wine tasters mention when describing Burgundy wines. Such is the way that subtle blueberry, raspberry, and strawberry

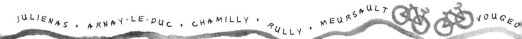

undertones of Côtes de Nuits reds became transformed into cassis-enriched reality in this most comforting of warm desserts.

To impart an essentially American-style fruit cobbler with a bit more French flair, I replaced the traditional crumbly, nut-studded topping with a more sophisticated lemon-laced sugar-cookie crust. French vanilla ice cream, of course, would be a welcome and appropriate embellishment.

> 1 quart fresh strawberries, hulled and quartered
> 1 pint fresh or frozen whole unsweetened blueberries
> 1 pint fresh or frozen whole unsweetened raspberries
> ⅓ cup sugar
> 3 tablespoons unbleached all-purpose flour
> ½ cup cassis

> COOKIE CRUST
> 1 cup (2 sticks) unsalted butter, at room temperature
> 1 cup sugar
> 1 egg
> 1 teaspoon vanilla extract
> 2 teaspoons grated lemon zest
> 1 cup unbleached all-purpose flour
> ½ teaspoon baking powder
> Pinch of salt

182

1. Preheat the oven to 375°F.

2. Combine all the berries, sugar, flour, and cassis in a large bowl, then spread it evenly into a 13 x 9-inch baking pan. Set aside.

3. Make the cookie crust: In a medium-size bowl, cream the butter and sugar with an electric mixer until smooth. Beat in the egg, vanilla, and lemon zest. Sift the flour, baking powder, and salt over the creamed mixture. Stir with a wooden spoon to incorporate the flour and make a semistiff, cookie type of batter.

4. Drop the cookie topping by tablespoonsful evenly over the top of the berry filling.

5. Bake the crisp until the top is light golden brown and the berry filling is bubbling, 45 to 50 minutes. Let the crisp cool for at least 15 minutes and serve it warm, with vanilla ice cream on top, if desired.

MAKES 8 SERVINGS

Pinot Noir Granité

Burgundians find it hard to resist cooking with their native wine, and this frozen pinot noir wins my vote as the most memorable and creative example of wine cookery I've experienced in my travels. It was savored with my cycling group at yet another one of our five-hour-long dining extravaganzas at the luxurious three-star Restaurant Lameloise in Chagny. Here, the Pinot Noir *Granité* was offered mid-meal in a small, crystal goblet as a palate-cleansing sorbet. My delight in securing the chef's recipe became complete when, en route home, I managed to scoop up a nifty little machine for making sorbets at Zabar's (a New York culinary emporium laden with other great gadgets and discount prices).

If you are ambitious enough to try to replicate a multicourse Burgundian feast in your own home, then this is definitely the recipe you'll want to make and serve as an intermezzo. If your

dining style tends to be more casual, serve the Pinot Noir *Granité* as a simple yet very chic dessert.

> ½ *cup sugar*
> ⅓ *cup water*
> 2½ *cups red Burgundy wine or American pinot noir*

1. Combine the sugar and water in a small saucepan and bring to a boil over medium-high heat, stirring to dissolve the sugar. When the liquid is clear and bubbling, remove from heat and let cool to room temperature.

2. Combine the wine with the syrup and then freeze the mixture into a *granité* according to the individual manufacturer's instructions on your ice cream machine. Bear in mind that the alcohol in a *granité* keeps it from freezing as solidly as a sorbet or ice cream. The results should taste like an oenophile's dream of a snow cone.

MAKES ABOUT 3 CUPS, SERVES 6

184

Café Chez Camille

Recently, the Burgundy bicycle trips have been commencing up in the fertile farmlands surrounding Arnay-le-Duc. The town boasts a great little regional museum devoted exclusively to table arts and the quirky but delightful restaurant/hotel Chez Camille, our home for the first night. Chez Camille just happens to be my idea of the perfect eclectic rural French hotel, and I especially love the restaurant's rustic greenhouse dining room

with the only open-to-view kitchen I've ever witnessed in all of France. I celebrated my birthday at Chez Camille one year, and the evening began with a menu consultation over an apéritif and *gougères* served in a cozy sideroom with a huge, roaring fire. The evening ended with this potent, *marc*-laced coffee, presented humorously with a straw. I should caution that this is the sort of nightcap that makes the recipient pray for either a designated driver or a room at the inn.

> 3 cups freshly brewed coffee
> ½ cup marc de Bourgogne or brandy
> 3 tablespoons sugar
> ½ cup heavy (or whipping) cream
> ½ teaspoon vanilla extract

Heat the coffee, *marc,* and sugar together in a small saucepan over medium heat until piping hot. Meanwhile, whip the cream and vanilla together until soft peaks form. Divide the coffee mixture between two glass mugs. Spoon or pipe the whipped cream lavishly over the top of each. Serve at once, with a straw if desired.

MAKES 2 SERVINGS

185

Index